HOW TO
TALK TO
ANYBODY

HOW TO TALK TO ANYBODY

LEARN THE SECRETS TO SMALL TALK, BUSINESS, MANAGEMENT,
SALES & SOCIAL SKILLS & HOW TO MAKE REAL FRIENDS

DEREK BORTHWICK

Dip.C.Hyp/NLP

DEDICATION

For Skye, Jamie and Adam.

"It matters not what we mean to communicate, but rather it is the way it is interpreted that creates the meaning"

Derek Borthwick

ABOUT THE AUTHOR

Derek Borthwick, *BSc. (Hons), Dip.C. Hyp/NLP*, is an expert in the mind and communication skills. He has over thirty years' experience in sales, distribution and marketing and has raised over a billion dollars in assets and has worked with some of the world's largest companies. He has lectured at top Scottish Universities and specialises in advanced communication, persuasion and influence methods. Derek gained a diploma in clinical hypnotherapy and is a certified master practitioner of neurolinguistic programming (NLP). He has a diploma in business coaching from the Henka Institute.

CONTENTS

PART ONE

The Secret Ingredients

Get Your Free Rapid Learning Accelerator Audio and Bonus Chapter at the End of Chapter 24

CHAPTER 1

What's the Difference

Many of us have seen those people who communicate easily and effortlessly. They seem to have a natural ability to speak to anyone, anytime, anywhere and in any situation. Many of us would love to have this charisma, charm and confidence and to be able to attract, draw people towards us and captivate them. This is not a natural ability that some people are born with, but is something that we can learn. Behind these "natural" communicators, a lot of practise has taken place. There have been many mistakes made and rectified, as these people have refined their art.

WHY IS THIS BOOK DIFFERENT?

This book is not a book of tips, it uses an entire brain approach to mastering how to talk to anybody. This does not mean there won't be suggestions you can adopt immediately. However, the focus in this book is away from a list of tips and towards giving you an insight into how people think and act so that you can develop powerful communication skills in any situation. Once you understand the methodology then you will be able to use this understanding rather than have to rely on a list of tips. Accompanying the book is an audio that will help program your mind to quicken the process.

Tips Don't Work

There is a big secret, and that is that tips don't work! If you have ever encountered somebody who struggles with their weight, you can see how ineffective tips can be. Try giving a tip "eat less and move more". and notice the reaction that you get. While on the surface this is a tip and it should make sense, it shows a lack of understanding of the deeper issues associated with weight control. Try saying to a smoker all you have to do is to stop buying cigarettes. Perhaps you could say to a drug addict, just say no. Notice the response that you get. While these are all tips, they are likely to fall on deaf ears. In each of these cases, don't you think that the person would have thought about this themselves? It is not the conscious part of them that is controlling this behaviour, it is the unconscious part and we'll be exploring this as we go through this book. It is, therefore, the author's opinion that tips on their own rarely work.

Now perhaps I should correct this. Using one tip at a time for someone who has a level of competence in a particular skill may work. Imagine that you are a highly competent public speaker and yet there is one thing that you do that detracts from your impact. Let's assume that you have the habit of pointing at the audience. Pointing at people is not a great thing to do as it unconsciously puts people at unease. In this situation, a tip would be appropriate and that would be to stop pointing and to use the palms of your hands. Using the palms of your hands creates openness and the impression of being trustworthy. In this case, a tip would work. The speaker could then just focus on this one thing at a time. However, imagine that you had never done any public speaking or presenting before and are given a series of tips to adopt. You would quickly become confused and feel overwhelmed.

Why Is This Approach Different?

In part one, we will look at the powerful principles of how people think and communicate. In part two of the book, we will look at how we can apply what we have learned in part one to enable you to communicate with anyone in any situation. The book is unique because it targets not only conscious learning but unconscious learning as well. The accompanying audio will target your unconscious mind. Details can be found at the end of Chapter 24 of the book. Simply find a quiet period, relax, and just let the audio drift past you and you let your mind wander. As the audio targets your unconscious mind, you will be unaware of the changes. They will be gradual and subtle the more that you play this audio daily.

In the Genes?

Some think that the ability to talk to anyone and to be an excellent communicator is determined by genetics and that some people are born with this ability. Let's explore what science says about this.

New research from the field of epigenetics shows us that genes are merely a blueprint and can be switched on or off by thoughts in the form of chemical messengers. Argue for your weakness and it's yours. Be careful what you wish for, it might just come true!

As we approach the end of the first chapter, you wonder why it is so short? There's a reason for this If I had called this an introduction or an epilogue, you probably wouldn't have read it. We are all wired similarly as we shall see. It's essential that we understand the approach we are going to use, why it is different and how you can prepare yourself for success.

You may have heard the phrase that we're all different. We are but just not that different. I'm excited to begin, so let's start.

CHAPTER 2

What's the Problem?

For many of us, speaking is a natural process that we do without thinking. It is often the act of thinking that impedes our ability to speak to people. Our speech is carried out beneath our level of conscious awareness and is automatic. If I were to ask you what muscles you contract in your mouth and how you shape your tongue to formulate the words, you wouldn't consciously know how we do this. The way that we form words remains constant. The variable is the context in which we deliver those words. Thinking can interfere with the unconscious process. Let's explore this.

Walking the Plank

Imagine that I was to place a plank of wood on the ground with a width of 24 inches or 60 centimetres. If you are able bodied and I was to ask you to walk across that plank of wood, you could probably do that relatively easily in most cases.

Now let's assume that I take the same plank of wood and raise it in the air. This time I place it between two buildings three storeys up and ask you to walk across the plank. Now it gets tricky. Many of you may say that you could now not do it. Yet earlier you were more than capable of walking across the plank of wood when it was placed on the ground. What has changed? The context has changed. When the plank is raised into the air, your brain has now assessed more variables and has assessed what could happen if things went wrong. Yet the very act of walking across the plank of wood from a physical point of view is exactly the same.

We see this same occurrence when we speak to people and the context changes. Many people, if introduced to a world leader, celebrity or the Queen, would become nervous. This could affect their speech and it wouldn't flow as if speaking to their spouse, friends, or children.

Feeling the Fear

So what is it that causes this nervousness and anxiety? Scientists believe we are only born with two fears. These are the fear of loud noises and the fear of falling. This would imply that all other fears that we've developed have been learned. What is it that is preventing people from being able to speak fluently and confidently? The answer is fear.

There is a useful acronym that corresponds to the letters FEAR. It is "future events appearing real" or "future expectations appearing real". We will look at reality and imagination in more detail in a later section when we look at the brain and mind. Let's return to our example of walking across the raised plank. Our fear response is triggered and the protective mechanism kicks in as the brain attempts to protect us. The brain has identified that there is a possibility that if we were to fall, we could either kill or seriously injure ourselves.

The same desire to protect ourselves occurs when we engage in public speaking, speaking with strangers, or to somebody in authority. Thoughts may occur such as "What if I say something stupid?" or perhaps "What if I can't think of anything to say?" We don't want to appear stupid. This stimulates the part of the autonomic nervous system responsible for stress. If we do not control this, then we have a runaway state, and panic can set in.

People who get nervous and enter a runaway state have a talent for using their imagination. They have just learned to use this talent in the wrong way!

Fear of Rejection

You already speak to more strangers than you may think. However, like many people, you may only speak to strangers when you need to. You may lack confidence or you may feel that you are not very good at it or could be better at it. In your mind, that it is true but is it. We will look at perception and reality and how to change it as we work our way through this book. If you can work on changing your mindset and how you feel about talking to strangers, it will open up a whole new world of opportunities for you. Even if you feel rejected, it is how you react to it that affects the outcome.

Laugh It Away

I have a friend who has a different view of life from most people. I learned from him to laugh away things that would affect most people. He finds it funny when someone doesn't like him! So much so he celebrates the fact and starts laughing! It is hilarious to observe, and he is right. It is only somebody else's perception, and it is never accurate, as we shall see when we explore how our brains and minds work.

Two Nerve Centres

We have an autonomic nervous system that runs below conscious awareness. Within this autonomic nervous system, there are two systems responsible for regulating the organs of the body in response to a stimulus (Fig.1). There is the parasympathetic nervous system and the sympathetic nervous system. The hypothalamus in the brain maintains homeostasis or balance between the two nervous systems.

The parasympathetic nervous system is stimulated when we are at rest, "the rest and digest state". The sympathetic nervous system is stimulated by the fear response at times of stress. When stressed, the amygdala sends a message to the hypothalamus. If overstimulated, it triggers the fight, flight, or freeze response. This prepares the body for fight or flight by increasing the blood flow to the large muscles and away from the extremities. Breathing becomes shallower, faster, higher, in the chest, and the heart rate increases. Non-essential systems shut down and peripheral vision together with hearing are reduced. We experience tunnel or foveal vision. The digestive and immune systems also shut down. This results in butterflies in the stomach. Now that we know what happens when somebody is stressed or nervous, we will see this manifest itself in the outward body's expression.

When in the resting stage, blood flow to the extremities is increased. This can cause a flushed look on the face, a fuller lower lip and deeper slower breathing. The pupils will be less dilated to allow for a wider field of view. If shaking hands with someone, the hand is often warm and not moist.

Homeostasis Is the Balance Between the Parasympathetic and Sympathetic Nervous System.

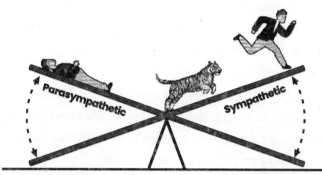

Rest, Heal and Digest –
Parasympathetic Nervous
System Stimulated

Fight, Flight or Freeze –
Sympathetic Nervous
System Stimulated

Fig.1

Compare this with someone that is nervous or stressed and there is less colour in the face. The language reflects this with the expression "white as a ghost". The breathing is also shallower and higher in the chest, and the lower lip is less full and paler. The hands are often cold to the touch and maybe moist too. You may notice "bad breath" as the person is in ketosis.

Why Did I Not Say That?

You may have had a situation where you have either been in a heated debate or argument or when somebody was shouting at you. You may have not have been able to think and know what to say and your voice may have tensed up. You may even have said some odd things. Then afterwards, as you calm down, you may have thought to yourself "I wish I had said that" as you replay the argument over again in your mind.

What has happened? Blood drained from the prefrontal cortex, shutting down your critical function. When this occurs, it makes it virtually impossible to learn anything or to focus on small things. It also makes it difficult to engage with other people, as the survival instincts kick in and this reflects our inability to remember things.

Many of us will have had the experience of being under stress and of trying to read a page in a book. We can read a passage repeatedly and it just won't go in. Why does this happen? This is because our critical brain has shut down.

We will explore this in more detail when we look at how the brain and mind work.

You Do It to Yourself

When coaching people, I often hear that public speaking, speaking to strangers, speaking in social or business situations makes people uncomfortable.

This is incorrect. The act of public speaking or speaking to strangers doesn't make you nervous or uncomfortable. You do it to yourself by choosing how you react to the situation. The brain is a data processing device that interprets external data and constructs a version of reality, as we shall see.

Where's the Instruction Manual

There is more to talking to people than at first thought. Imagine that you had just been given a new piece of electrical equipment or have downloaded some software for your computer. If there was no instruction manual, then we have to learn by trial and error. We might never work it out and may never discover the shortcuts.

I have underfloor heating in my downstairs bathroom, which makes the tiles nice and warm. Recently the thermostat broke. Having mastered how to use the old thermostat, I immediately went to the shop to replace it with the same model. To my dismay, they no longer made that model. It had been superseded by a new one. The new thermostat was all singing and all dancing and linked to my phone by Wi-Fi. Only basic instructions came with the new one. Neither the electrician nor I could fathom out how to connect to the Wi-Fi and how to programme the thermostat. We ended up pressing many buttons and being greeted with various beeping sounds. You could imagine my sense of frustration with this device.

Think about our brains and minds. As we enter the world, nobody says, "Welcome to the world and here is your instruction manual". We try this and that and make lots of mistakes along the way. Some of us never truly master the workings of the brain and mind. Think about how much easier it would be if an instruction manual had been given to us. How useful would that have been?

In this book, you will receive this instruction manual, but in an easy and fun format. It may seem basic in places, but we need the basics to build on this as we learn how to communicate effortlessly and easily. It is key to have an understanding of these basics before we move forward.

CHAPTER 3

Three Brains & Two Minds

Most people think that they have one brain. We actually have three "brains", each one performing specialised functions. This three brain model became known as the "triune model" from the work of Paul MacLean. (Fig.2) While there have been further refinements, it serves as a good metaphor.

The three brains are:

1. Reptilian, Stem Brain or Paleocortex
2. Mammalian, Midbrain, or Limbic System
3. Human or neocortex brain

Understanding the Triune

The reptilian or paleocortex filters all the incoming messages and handles most of the fight, flight or freeze responses. It is also responsible for some of the very basic and strong primitive emotions. Its primary responsibility is not with thinking, but with survival. When driving a car, if somebody suddenly jumps out in front of the car, we don't want to think about applying the brakes. It's done automatically for us by the reptilian brain. The reptilian brain does not process details well, it only passes along big obvious chunks of concrete data.

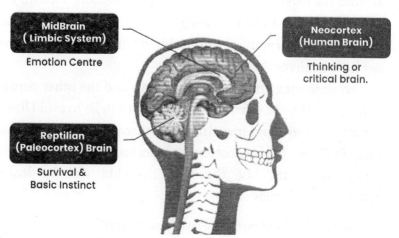

MidBrain
(Limbic System)

Emotion Centre

Neocortex
(Human Brain)

Thinking or
critical brain.

Reptilian
(Paleocortex) Brain

Survival &
Basic Instinct

Fig. 2

The midbrain, also known as the mammalian brain or the limbic system, is sometimes referred to as the chimp brain. It makes sense of and attaches meaning to situations and is the emotional centre. It is the honest brain it answers first and honestly.

The neocortex is the outer part of the brain responsible for critical thinking and logic and is responsible for analysing. It will critique and analyse a proposition or proposal. It is the least well informed and is the last to know. This is the lying brain and will add justification to our behaviour, however irrational it may be. The information has to pass through the reptilian brain, to the midbrain and onto the neocortex to be analysed and critiqued. Let's use an example of how the three brains might work.

Imagine that somebody appears wearing an outfit that is shocking, inappropriate and not to your taste. The reptilian brain immediately processes this unexpected and unpredicted change as a mild shock. The limbic brain then puts context around the experience and it creates an emotion. This may be disbelief, shock, horror or even humour. The neocortex then analyses the information, and the inner voice may say, "Do they not have a mirror in their house?"

The neocortex attempts to protect us and the other person, as harsh truths can offend. It may cause us to lie to avoid losing a friend and to avoid upsetting the other person by protecting their feelings. The neocortex has worked out that the lie is beneficial to us, but the true thoughts will be leaked nonverbally. We may say:

"I love your new outfit. It really suits you!"

However, this may not be what we are really thinking? In business, we may say to our boss:

"I really like the new sales strategy for our company. It sounds very exciting."

However, do we mean it? If we are saying this to others, would it be fair to assume that they may say this to us too? The neocortex is thus the lying brain. It justifies our behaviour. For example:

"It doesn't matter if I steal from them, as they have plenty of money anyway."

Remember, for something to be interpreted as true, it does not have to be true, just plausible. This is important and we will explore this in more detail going forward. When someone says I really value your honest opinion, what they really mean is,

"I value your opinion as long as it is similar to mine and does not offend me."

It is important to remember this.

Working with the Brain

Our brain makes its best guestimate of reality based on the data entering it and is constantly refining the model. If reality is as predicted, then the information is processed at an unconscious level. If something unexpected happens in the environment, this may be raised to consciousness to be processed, assessed, and evaluated.

Let's imagine walking down the street on our way to work on a Monday morning. As we walk down the street suddenly, we see a man dressed as a pirate. This would be unusual and would not be expected or predicted. Immediately, this is raised to consciousness. The brain has to make sense of this new information. Our reptilian survival brain kicks in and decides if the pirate is a friend or foe. Next, the mammalian or limbic system puts context around the experience and produces an emotion. It may be laughter, curiosity, or anger.

Finally, the information passes to the neocortex. This is the moment that we have all had after witnessing something unusual when we try to make sense of it. We often speak to ourselves and say, "Why would somebody be dressed like a pirate in the middle of Edinburgh on a Monday morning?"

Understanding the Reptile

The reptilian brain works based on:

- *Is something a threat or a danger?*
- *Is something new and exciting?*

- *If it is new, get to the point quickly and make it simple*
- *If it is not new and unexpected, then ignore it*

What Does This Mean for Conversation?

- *If you are boring, you will be ignored*
- *If you are a threat, you will be ignored*
- *If something is complicated, it will be ignored*

What to Do?

- *Pique another person's interest*
- *Avoid being seen as a threat, intellectually or socially*
- *Make things simple to understand*
- *Build rapport rapidly*

Working With the Reptile and the Chimp

When we meet somebody for the first time, the brain is assessing whether they are a friend or foe. It then tries to reference the experience and an emotional response is generated as it tries to provide some context. Finally, we critically evaluate the information to make sense of it and formulate our opinion.

Yet, think about what happens in a typical business situation. First, we try to appeal to the critical brain and try to "logic" somebody into a decision. Then we hope they feel good about us. Finally, we hope that they have not perceived us as a threat. This approach is the inverse to how our brains work.

Let's use an example to illustrate this. Suppose that you are looking for a partner to form an intimate relationship with. Let's assume that you are in a bar or a nightclub and you see somebody that you like. Imagine walking up to that person and presenting them with a list of ten reasons to go out with you on a date. Having presented the list to them, you then explain logically why they should go out with you. How successful would this approach be? Exactly, although bizarrely enough, it might work in the odd case, as a pattern interrupt. A pattern interrupt is where something unusual occurs that was not predicted in the brain's model. In most cases, people would just think of this as unusual behaviour and yet, is this not what we do in conversations?

TWIN MIND MASTERY

Let's explore how our mind works or more specifically, how our twin minds work. We don't have to be mind experts, we just need a basic understanding which will assist us when we want to speak to anyone, anytime and in any situation. Think about driving a car. We don't have to understand what all the wiring and mechanical components do but we do need to understand the controls. Let's get started.

Our minds consist of two components. We have the conscious mind, which is our critical mind. This can only hold limited pieces of information in our conscious awareness at any one point in time. We also have the unconscious mind which controls the activities that go on out with of our conscious awareness. Let's explore these now.

The Conscious Mind

George Miller, a cognitive psychologist, published a paper in 1956. It is often referred to and used to argue the case that the human mind can hold 7 plus or minus 2 pieces of information in conscious awareness. The 7 plus or minus 2 model serves as a suitable metaphor, but it is more complicated than this. The brain organises information in chunks. Think about your telephone number. How do you remember it? If someone asks for our telephone number, we have a pattern and grouping of numbers that we use to remember our number.

Let's suppose your telephone number is 0131 234 5678. The grouping of numbers here is 3 3 4. Now try relaying your number in a different grouping of numbers and notice how difficult it is.

If repeated back in a different grouping of numbers, it can sometimes be confusing. This shows how the brain organises information into groups or chunks. We have a limit to how much information we can process consciously before getting confused. Hypnotists, magicians and pickpockets are aware of this, and use this to their advantage to confuse us.

The conscious mind, therefore, has a very limited bandwidth of data that is brought to consciousness. We do, however, have control over the conscious mind, and we can choose what we want to be conscious of. We can move our consciousness and awareness around. For example, you are now aware of the feelings in your left foot and you can now feel the clothing against your skin. You are now aware of the temperature in the room. There are millions of bits of data coming in and yet we are not aware of most of it.

Our conscious mind is the least well informed and the last to know. It is our lying brain. It lies frequently and often. It justifies our behaviours and the behaviour of others based on our own set of values and beliefs. If the new information or a suggestion fits in with our beliefs and values, then is accepted. If it doesn't, our conscious critical mind rejects it. Let's look at our conscious mind in more detail.

The conscious mind is the critical part of the brain and evaluates information and solves puzzles. It is our higher thinking brain and protects us by analysing information that we have come across previously and putting it in a higher level context.

While the lower parts of the brain are operating by instinct, the higher part of the brain critically analyses suggestions and statements made. For example, imagine that I told you that a house had a special magnetic field that would prevent you from getting injured if you placed your hand in a pot of boiling water. Your conscious, critical mind would hopefully think that this is highly unlikely. I would hope that you would seek more information and some proof before engaging in this activity.

Now you may think that is an extreme example. However, you would be surprised at some suggestions that have been given over the years and accepted as true because the critical mind has been bypassed. When looking at the suppression of the critical mind, we are moving into the world of hypnosis. This is a big topic and beyond this book.

The Unconscious Mind

The unconscious mind controls the vast majority of the processes and behaviours that we have. These go on at an unconscious level. It is the engine room, and it controls our breathing, heart rate, blood sugar level, body temperature together with digestion and the healing process. There are only two processes that operate unconsciously that we can override consciously and then only to a limited extent. That is our blinking and our breathing.

The unconscious mind processes around 40 million bits of data per second. That is a big difference compared to the conscious mind, which processes around 40 bits of data per second. The unconscious mind, therefore, is a million times more powerful, according to Dr Bruce Lipton.

The unconscious mind always answers first and answers honestly, and if we watch for the nonverbal signals, we see people leak their thoughts through their nonverbal actions. These show their true thoughts and feelings. The outer expression reflects the inner thought. This is the basis for understanding Body Language and is explored in great detail in the author's book "Body Language How to Read Any Body".

There are special ways to communicate with the unconscious mind. The unconscious mind does not critique or analyse but takes things literally. Its job is to keep us safe and to regulate our bodily functions. It responds to imagery, repetition, emotion and stories.

The accompanying audio that comes with this book has been specially recorded to speak to the unconscious mind. It is highly recommended that you listen to this audio for 30 days to help access the unconscious mind and to speed up the learning process.

We can think of the unconscious mind a bit like a junction box. We have millions and millions of bits of data coming in via our senses, and yet we are only aware of a tiny amount of it in our conscious awareness. Much of this processing takes place by the unconscious mind. We can decide what 5 to 9 switches we want turned on at any point in time. Let's switch one on. You are now aware of the sensation in your mouth.

Who's Driving the Bus?

Think of the conscious mind as the driver of the bus. The driver decides how fast to drive the bus, decides when it's going to stop and in what direction to point the bus. Think of the unconscious mind as the bus. It is the engine and all the hardware that makes sure that the bus keeps moving in the direction that the driver points the bus in.

The conscious mind can override our behaviour to a certain extent. However, it takes a lot of effort. Consider if you are out on a date for dinner. Most of us want to give the best possible impression. We make sure when eating that we don't exhibit any bad habits or poor etiquette. We make sure not to speak with our mouths full. Our conscious mind is overriding our natural behaviours, and this takes effort. However, as we become more familiar with somebody, we have less conscious control over our natural patterns of behaviour. The conscious mind thinks about other things, and our etiquette may slip.

This may be the same with your speaking and communication skills. For some of us, we may muddle through speaking to strangers or presenting, but only if we concentrate very hard.

For many, however, it just doesn't feel natural. This book aims to make this a natural process.

Faulty Bus

Let's return to the bus and suppose that the bus has a fault with it and it is veering off to the left-hand side. This could represent the challenge that we may have with talking, presenting, or speaking with people. If the bus is constantly veering off to the left-hand side, then the driver has to constantly correct the bus to make sure that it continues to travel in a straight line. If the driver forgets to do this and is not paying attention, then the bus will veer off to the left-hand side and ultimately crash. We need to get into the control area of the bus to correct the fault that is causing it to veer to the left-hand side.

Imagine that all the controls dials and switches that we needed to change and fiddle with are inside a large room and operate the bus remotely. Now, ideally, we would just like to walk into this control room and make the adjustments. However, there's a problem. For security, a guard has been placed at the entrance.

This engine room represents your unconscious mind, and the guard represents your conscious or critical mind. If we go to the guard and explain that we want to go into the engine room and if we can't persuade him or he does not believe this to be in the best interest of the bus, then he won't let us in. Equally, if we can't get into the room to adjust the controls, then the bus is going to carry on veering to the left-hand side. If we want to get past the guard, we have to make sure that his awareness has been suppressed. We can do this in several ways.

We can either distract the guard so that he is not paying attention and then sneak in through the door or we can wait until the guard is asleep, and then go in and start altering the switches, dials and the settings. Once we are inside the control room with all the levers dials, we can make minor changes that are needed and do so without the guard spotting them when he does his security walk round. This means that we have to visit this room regularly to make small, subtle changes.

This is exactly what the accompanying audio does, which is to get past the guard and make changes without your conscious mind knowing. The audio needs to be used frequently.

Sweet Dreams

The brain cannot tell the difference between something vividly imagined and something experienced. It's the same parts of the brain that light up when measured using fMRI scanning. To illustrate this, let's draw on some of the research. A group of volunteers were divided into two groups. The first group was asked to play a simple sequence of piano notes each day for five consecutive days. Their brains were scanned each day in the region connected to the finger muscles. The second group was asked to imagine playing the notes instead and also had their brains scanned each day.

The changes in the brain in those who imagined playing the piano were the same as in those who played the piano. This proves that our brain doesn't distinguish real from imaginary! It explains why we can feel nervous or stressed without doing anything. The brain imagines a reality that doesn't exist.

Getting Nervous

The stress response has developed in humans to give us the ability to fight, flight, or flee when faced with danger. While this is very useful, if you are being chased by a dangerous wild animal, it's not useful if you want to talk to someone. The response depends on the degree of absorption and vividness of someone's imagination. Sometimes, this can elicit some extreme responses. For some people, even mentioning climbing up to a height can cause an adverse reaction. Simply imagining fingernails being scraped on a blackboard can cause a response in others. For others, simply imagining speaking at certain events or certain people can bring on anxiety or unease.

Einstein Imagination

Einstein knew all about the importance of imagination. Imagination is powerful and nothing in this world would exist if someone had not imagined it at some point. If we think about a bridge, for it to exist, somebody at some point had to imagine it.

The Other You

If you play golf, drive a car, ride a bicycle, ski or play a musical instrument competently, then who is controlling this? You may think that is a bizarre question and answer it with, *"Well, it's me, of course"*. However, which "me" is it? There is the "you" that you are aware of, but there is also the other "you" that you are not aware. The unconscious mind is the part that you are unaware of and it controls over ninety five per cent of what we do daily. We could think of this as an iceberg with the vast proportion of the iceberg hidden from view.

This other you controls your communication when you are speaking to other people. This is done automatically. Often it is when you start to over-analyse, thought interference occurs and that is when things go wrong. This may have been when you have felt awkward and said the wrong things.

This conscious mind interference can often cause problems. When you hear of artists or musicians or sportspeople "being in the zone", they are performing at their peak without having to think about it. Let me share with you a short story to illustrate how conscious thought can interfere with unconscious processes.

I injured my knee while skiing years ago. I was skiing down a very steep mountain ski run at Glencoe in Scotland called the "Flypaper". This is a run that you just don't fall on! I'm a competent skier and I was skiing down the run one day when suddenly, I had a thought. I began to wonder what it is that I am doing to turn as I was doing this unconsciously. In that split moment, I lost control and ended up tumbling to the bottom. This was an incredibly frightening experience, as there was no way to stop. This momentary intervention from my conscious mind resulted in a snapped cruciate ligament.

If you play golf, you will be well aware of the battle that goes on in between your ears with mind interference and the little voice.

If you're still not convinced that there is another you, why do you refer to the other you? You may have heard people say, "*I'm really annoyed at myself*". Think about that. What does that mean? Who is annoyed and with whom?

Often, experts and sportspeople perform so much unconsciously that it's quite difficult for them to coach. This is because they don't know what they do. They do it automatically. We see this with musicians too.

Learning to Learn

Think about a time when you learned a new skill. It may have been learning to play a musical instrument, learning to play golf, ski or drive. You may even have tried to learn a foreign language. The learning phase can be quite frustrating. Which part of you is doing this? Well, it's the part that you are aware of, the conscious mind, and it doesn't seem to do it very well.

I enjoy playing the electric guitar and when trying to learn a new solo, it can be incredibly frustrating as my fingers won't go where I want them to go. However, I have found that practising in small periods and then having a break seems to help speed up the learning. If I leave it a few days and then return, it seems to be easier. It's almost as if the brain is wiring up while I'm sleeping or away from the musical instrument.

When learning something new, the conscious mind is doing this, and it is the part that we are aware of. Let's look now at how we learn and how the skills that you will learn from this book will become automatic if you follow the process.

The Four Stages of Learning

When learning a new skill, we go through four stages of learning and these are listed below.

1. Unconscious Incompetence. We are unaware that we don't know how to do something

2. Conscious Incompetence. We are aware that we don't know how to do something

3. Conscious Competence. We can now do something but must concentrate, and it is not yet natural

4. Unconscious Competence. The skill is now hard-wired and we can do it without thinking

Learning from Chicken Sexers

Separating the egg producing female from male chicks has important commercial value and is a skill called "sexing". The best chicken sexers come from Japan. Separating males from females is difficult, as both look identical to the untrained eye. The training method involves training the brain through trial and error until it becomes an unconscious process. Something that can seem impossible to begin with soon becomes an unconscious, competent process.

When learning a new skill, it is important to realise the four stages of learning. When going through this book, there may be things you do, are aware of and do well, and there will be things you are less aware of. The key is to break things down and practice them. Trying to learn everything all at once can cause a feeling of being overwhelmed.

Sometimes you can go straight from unconscious incompetence to unconscious competence. If you think about putting your hand in a fire for the first time, you realise that it burns you. This is "one stage learning" and you don't have to keep repeating the activity to know that this is a painful and dangerous thing to do.

The more we practise things then the more they will go from conscious competence to unconscious competence. The best way to learn things is to break them down into small bite-sized chunks.

Eating the Toblerone

A Toblerone chocolate or candy bar, if you're not familiar with it, is a triangular chocolate bar that comprises of triangular pieces of very hard chocolate connected to make a long triangular shaped chocolate bar. The chocolate is very hard because of the triangular shape and pointy edges.

If I was to give you a Toblerone chocolate or candy bar and ask you to put it in your mouth and bite into it, it would be painful to bite. However, if we break the Toblerone down into small triangular chunks and eat one piece at a time, then it becomes much easier.

Using the Toblerone analogy, the more that we can break things down into simple pieces then the easier it is for us to learn. As we learn, those pieces become gelled together just like the Toblerone bar until eventually we have mastered the skill and have a full Toblerone.

CHAPTER 4

Open Hearted

The heart is constantly responding to "orders" sent by the brain as neural signals. However, the heart sends more signals to the brain than the brain sends to the heart. Heart signals have a significant effect on the brain and influence emotions together with attention, perception, memory and problem solving. The heart communicates to the brain in four major ways:

1. Neurologically (via transmission of nerve impulses)
2. Biochemically (via hormones and neurotransmitters)
3. Biophysically (via pressure waves)
4. Energetically (via electromagnetic field interactions)

All these communication methods affect brain activity. Research from the Heartmath Institute shows that the messages that the heart sends to the brain can also affect performance. The heart is the most powerful source of electromagnetic energy in the human body, producing the largest rhythmic electromagnetic field of the body's organs. The heart's electrical field is about sixty times greater in amplitude than the electrical activity generated by the brain. The magnetic field produced by the heart is more than a hundred times greater in strength than the field generated by the brain. This can be detected up to three feet away from the body and has been verified using SQUID-based magnetometers.

Evidence now supports the idea that a subtle yet influential electromagnetic or "energetic" communication system operates just below our conscious level of awareness. The results of these experiments have concluded that the nervous system acts as a type of antenna, which is tuned to and responds to the magnetic fields produced by the hearts of other individuals.

This energetic communication ability can be enhanced, resulting in a much deeper level of nonverbal communication, understanding and connection between people. Energetic communication takes place in animals, too. Farmers have observed cattle and sheep facing the same way when grazing. The Heartmath Institute conducted an experiment showing heart synchronisation between a young boy and his dog and between a woman and her horse.

Having an ability to sense what other people are feeling is an important factor that allows us to connect or communicate with them. The smoothness of any interaction is enhanced by the establishment of spontaneous entrainment, which is explained in the next section.

When people are engaged in deep conversation, synchronisation takes place with their movements, postures, vocal pitch, speaking rates, and length of pauses between responses. It is like there is a dance occurring. In addition, their physiology synchronises too. Let's look at the scientific explanation for this.

SWINGING PENDULUMS

In 1666, the Dutch physicist, Christian Huygens, discovered that the pendulum frequencies of two clocks mounted on the same wall or board became synchronised to each other. He surmised that the vibrations of air molecules would transmit small amounts of energy from one pendulum to the other and synchronise them to a common frequency.

However, when the pendulums were placed on different surfaces, the effect disappeared. The transmitting medium was the vibrating board or wall. The stronger "oscillator" locks the weaker into its frequency. When both oscillating bodies have equally strong energy, both systems move toward each other. The faster system slows down and the slower system speeds up until they lock into a common movement.

Entrainment

The synchronisation of pendulums can be explained by entrainment. Entrainment is a process through which independent systems interact with each other. When two signals are close to each other in frequency, they fall into a single frequency, just like when the pendulums swung in synchronisation.

The phenomenon also extends to the biological world, where examples include those of synchronising fireflies and in humans with the resetting of the body clocks by sunlight (circadian entrainment). The "entraining" signal can be from inside the body or from outside.

Have you ever walked down the street deep in conversation with someone and then looked down and noticed that your footsteps were totally in sync? This is an example of entrainment. Entrainment is an unconscious process and breathing can become entrained with the beat of the music.

Experiments have shown that when individuals interact socially, for example in conversation, the rhythms of their actions become entrained. It is not merely enough being in the same room, there has to be mutual attention for this to occur. This is implying that there is some sort of connection that connects people and the key ingredient is mutual attention to each other.

CHAPTER 5

Your Plastic Brain

Your Super Computer

It has been estimated that the brain comprises around 100 billion neurons. David Eagleman in his book "Livewired" explains that these neurons are connected as a neural network and the total number of connections between the neurons in your brain is around 0.2 quadrillion. It is an impossible number to visualise. There are twenty times more connections in a cubic millimetre of cortical tissue than there are people on the planet.

This circuitry is constantly being changed and altered in response to the demands of the environment and the capabilities of our body. We can think of the brain as a living community of trillions of cells forming connections with each other. Whenever we learn a new piece of information or a new skill, the interconnection between the cells in the network changes in response to this. This constant rewiring is an ongoing process.

This map of the world that we have is constantly evolving as the terrain changes. The idea of a system that changes in response to external events and keeps its new shape led the psychologist William James to coin the term plasticity. This has led to the term brain plasticity or neuroplasticity, which is the term that is used in neuroscience to refer to the brain remoulding itself throughout our lives.

To illustrate an extreme version of neuroplasticity, we can look at the case of a child which we will call Matthew, who was suffering from seizures. These seizures became worse and eventually were taking place every two minutes. There was only one known treatment for Matthew's condition and that was surgical removal of half of the brain known as a hemispherectomy.

After the removal of half of Matthew's brain, he couldn't walk or speak and was incontinent. However, remarkably after daily physical therapy and language therapy, his brain began rewiring. Matthew cannot use his right hand properly and walks with a slight limp, but otherwise, there is little sign that he has had half of his brain removed and he lives a normal life. Many people when meeting Matthew have no idea that he only has half a brain.

How could this possibly have occurred? The remaining part of Matthews' brain has rewired itself to take over the missing functions. We can think of neurons as growing like trees, with each branch connecting to other neurons. This gives us an important rule which has been incorporated into neurolinguistic programming (software for the mind). This is that neurons that fire together wire together. This flexibility for rewiring can be seen in animals, too. Faith the dog was born without forelimbs, and yet she grew from being unable to walk, to walking on her two hind legs like a human.

Teaching an Old Dog New Tricks

We have looked at how Matthew's brain rewired itself to give him a relatively normal life. You may well be thinking, well, this is all very well with young people, but can we get the brain to rewire if people are older? Let's explore this further.

An engineer by the name of Destin Sandlin was given as a present from a friend a bicycle that had been altered so that when he turned the handlebars to the left, the bicycle would turn to the right and vice versa. Destin was unsure if he could ride the bicycle. While cognitively he understood the instructions to operate the bicycle with the reversed steering system, the old patterns of behaviour had been so ingrained that he was unsure if he could do it.

However, after several weeks of daily practise Destin became quite good at it. This is because he was constantly getting feedback in the form of data for his brain to interpret. He learned that if he turned the handlebars the wrong way that he would crash. His brain had learned a new schema (pattern of behaviour). When Destin returned to riding a regular bicycle, he found he couldn't ride it. However, this was short-lived and with a little practise he could ride both bicycles.

I like to think of this as walking through a dense field of corn. There is no path to begin with, and walking through the corn is difficult. However, after repeatedly walking down the same downtrodden corn, a path emerges, and it becomes easier each time we walk down it. That doesn't mean that we can't start another path, it just means that when we do, it is often difficult until the second path emerges.

It means that we always have choices and while one path of corn may become overgrown; it is always there.

Do you think that if Mathew can learn to talk, speak and live a relatively normal life and Destin can learn to ride a bicycle with the steering reversed, that perhaps you can rewire your brain to be a great communicator? I think so.

Hungry for Data

We still don't fully understand the workings of the brain, but we know it is a data processing biological machine that is incredible at taking external data and extracting patterns from that data. From those patterns, the brain assigns meaning. With this meaning, we have a subjective experience. Whatever information is fed to the brain it responds and will extract what it can, as long as the data has a structure and reflects something important about the outside world. Let's look at an example of this.

Two year old Ben Underwood stopped seeing out of his left eye. Tragically, he was diagnosed with retinal cancer in both eyes. This caused surgeons to remove both his eyes. However, by the time Ben was seven years old, he had devised an unexpected and very useful technique. He made clicks with his mouth and listened for the returning echoes. This has enabled him to locate people, parked cars, etc. He developed echo locating and was bouncing sound waves off objects in the environment. His brain had learned to interpret this data and to make sense of the patterns of data coming in. There have been other instances of people showing echolocation. This is not just a technique that is restricted to a few people, it's just that most of us do not have the patience or motivation to learn it.

Let's have a look at the brain interpreting random data. Have a look at the following text and see if you can read it.

7H15 M3554G3 53RV35 7O PR0V3 H0W 0UR M1ND5 C4N DO 4M4Z1NG 7H1NG5! 1MPR3551V3 7H1NG5! 1N 7H3 B3G1NN1NG 17 WA5 H4RD BU7 N0W, 0N 7H15 LIN3 Y0UR M1ND 1S R34D1NG 17 4U70M471C4LLY W17H0U7 3V3N 7H1NK1NG 4B0U7 17, B3 PROUD! 0NLY C3R741N P30PL3 C4N R3AD 7H15!

Learning Communication

Think about how you learned, and continue to learn to communicate with other people. You will have been in different social interactions and each time your brain received feedback about what worked and what didn't. You will have learned that different jokes work in different situations and that different approaches work with different people. We have found that we can use similar strategies in similar situations with similar people and expect similar results.

We can adopt these different schemas (patterns of behaviour) in different situations and rely on social feedback to change our approach. We may have told a joke that was funny in one environment and that didn't go down very well in another one. We are always learning and even the professionals get it wrong and we shall now see.

Football Disaster

In the city of Glasgow in Scotland, there are two big football (soccer) teams, Rangers and Celtic. I remember attending a charity event where there was a particular allegiance to one of the Glasgow football (soccer) teams. This was years ago when there was more freedom of expression accepted. The room was full of men and the guest speaker was a former referee who had refereed many of the Celtic and Rangers games. There was a lot of alcohol flowing and while the language from the guest speaker was colourful and choice and many of the stories were close to the bone! He was, however, extremely funny. I remember leaving and thinking what a fantastic speaker he was and how much I enjoyed the evening.

Fast forward a month and I was attending an industry charity Christmas lunch. When I found out that the speaker was the same speaker that I'd seen before, I was waxing lyrical to the people around me, mentioning that I'd seen him a month earlier and how funny he was. This time the event was at lunchtime and was a mixed audience and not all male. As his language had been quite colourful at the previous evening's event, I assumed he would tone it down to fit in with the lunchtime setting. The lunchtime event was more professional and there was little alcohol consumption taking place.

When the guest speaker stood up to deliver his speech, I sat back and prepared to enjoy the speech. As he began delivering his speech, I was stunned to hear him deliver the same speech word for word with all the expletives! He was greeted with a stony silence. Everyone was cringing. I couldn't believe that it was the same speaker that I had heard previously getting such a different reaction. This just goes to show the importance of context, and I'm sure that his brain rewired and learned a lot from that experience.

CHAPTER 6

Reality Really

We discovered in the previous chapter that the brain is a data hungry machine that will interpret data as long as it is relevant to the environment. We have also seen that it can rewire and constantly does. Let's continue to discover more in our instruction manual.

Let's look at reality. What is it and do we all have the same reality? Some of you may wonder why there is a focus on reality. This may seem philosophical. However, for us to be successful and to be great communicators, we must have a good grasp on what it is and the findings may surprise you.

It's Personal

Each of us has our version of reality. We construct this by the brain filtering the data coming into our brain through the primary senses. All data is generalised, distorted, and some deleted, and we form our version of reality from this. We never actually experience full reality, just our version of it. This is our map of the world. This explains why we all like different music, food, holidays or vacations.

Therefore, we need to understand reality if we are going to learn how to hack into it.

Is it Real or Not?

For many, the sound of fingernails being dragged over a blackboard is unpleasant. Others may not like the sound of hands being rubbed against a balloon. For people who dislike either of these, simply vividly imagining the experience can cause real discomfort. The better the imagination is engaged in the experience, then the more profound the effect will be. FMRI scanning of the brain shows that the same parts of the brain are activated when something is vividly imagined and when actually experienced, and we have seen that with the piano playing experiment earlier in the book. This may seem a hard concept to accept, and to illustrate this, we must enter the world of hypnosis.

An exploration of hypnosis shows that reality can be hijacked and overridden. The mind can be accessed under hypnosis, so much so that if a coin is placed on the skin, a blister can develop on removal if a posthypnotic suggestion is given to that effect. Dave Elman is one of the father figures of hypnosis. Elman trained medical professionals and dentists on how to use hypnosis for medical procedures. Elman would ask the dentists in his training classes to come forward, one after another, to be hypnotised. While under hypnosis, another dentist would probe the gingival, very sensitive, area of the mouth with a sharp dental probe. The dentist under hypnosis would feel no pain.

The Big Filter

We create our reality by filtering the data that comes in through our primary senses. The brain makes its best interpretation of this data and with it a guesstimate of reality. Yes, that is correct. We are not seeing what is out there but rather the brain's best guesstimate of what is there.

This is a hard concept for many to accept. However, as we go through this section, I will show you how you can satisfy this for yourself. The brain constructs reality not by what we are seeing, hearing or feeling but by what it expects to see, hear and feel. These expectations are based on all prior experiences and memories. The model is constructed and based on what has worked in the past.

If the brain's predicted reality is disrupted, it may take more time to process the data or more attention may be given to this unpredicted reality. If everything goes as anticipated with no surprises, the visual system will miss much of what's going on around us. Think of driving home. You probably remember little about the journey home unless something unusual occurs. If while driving home a lion darted across the road, this would be an unexpected, unpredicted event and would be raised to awareness for processing. The incident would be remembered. The lion would be a pattern interrupt. This can explain how something can be so controversial or outrageous, to begin with, and, through repetition, becomes accepted as the norm and, in many cases, not even noticed. The novelty factor quickly fades.

The biggest illusion is that reality exists and that we all have the same reality. Before you discount this let's explore this in more detail. We have seen we don't see with eyes but rather with our brains. We don't hear with our ears, but with our brains. The light that enters through our eyes accounts for only about 20 per cent of the image that we are seeing. The rest of the image is created based on a predictive mechanism of patterns and historical learnings. Now, this will seem a tough concept to grasp and many think well, of course, reality is real. I can see it! However, we don't know if what we're seeing is the same as what somebody else is seeing?

Let's use television as an example to illustrate the point. The television set forms television pictures from picking up waves that have been broadcast. When we go into a department store to buy a television, we may look at each one to see which has the best picture. The television program is identical for each television set, but each television processes the information slightly differently to create a picture. As humans, we're a bit like this. We see the same piece of information but we process it differently.

Consider our television sets again and let's assume that they are both tuned to different news channels broadcasting at the same time. One television is picking up the signal from one channel while the other television picks up a different news channel. Both signals are being broadcast as waves. However the TV's tuning will determine which news channel is being picked up. While both news channels may agree on the major event of the day, there will be differences in what they choose to report and the message associated with it. They will therefore agree on some detail but differ on others. You only have to look at different news channels in different parts of the world to see that there are different perspectives. In addition, sports channels are also broadcasting, but those were not being picked up. This is akin to the limits of our awareness. It is the same with humans. We are not aware of everything that is going on and are only forming an interpretation of the events, not what actually happened.

This is a really important concept to grasp because once you get it, the world starts to make more sense and explains why people react in the way that they do. Now some of you may still find this difficult to accept, so let's have a look at a couple of examples that you can use to prove this to yourself.

As discussed, we don't see everything that is out there. We see an interpretation of what the brain thinks is out there, and then the brain fills in the gaps. Many people have had the situation when they've been hunting around the house for their keys. Then, the moment that they are pointed out, they magically come into view. This is a negative hallucination and is an example of a deep, hypnotic phenomenon.

Our brains are data processing machines and will always try to attach meaning to seemingly random data. This explains why when you look up at the clouds, you will often see a face. The brain is constantly trying to make sense of data. In the absence of external stimuli it will begin hallucinating. Solitary confinement in complete darkness was seen as a punishment, and people began hallucinating.

The Camera Never Lies

Let's look at an example of how you can verify that the brain works as a predictive mechanism for yourself. Don't do this exercise if you're driving a car and only do this if it is safe to do. Pick a point in the distance and start nodding your head up and down while looking straight ahead. Pay attention to the image that you see. Is it moving or shaking? It's probably pretty static, isn't it? Now take your camera out and focus it on the same spot that you were looking at. Start moving it up and down by turning your wrist as if you were nodding your head. Press the record button to record the video and then play it back. What did you notice? The image is bouncing around all over the place on the video, isn't it? You may have seen this if you're watching footage of reporters or people moving with cameras, particularly going back to old analogue footage before image stabilisation was available in cameras.

This shows that we're not seeing what is going on, but the brain's prediction. If you're still not convinced, let's have a look at another example.

The Vanishing Cross

Only do this exercise if it is safe to do so and do not do this while driving. Find a piece of blank white paper, A4 or letter size, and a pen or a pencil. Now draw a small cross of about 1 centimetre or 1/2 an inch in the centre of the white piece of paper. Hold the piece of paper at eye level and at arm's length in front of you. Now look at the cross and fix your gaze on the cross. Keep looking at the cross and without moving your eyes, move the paper to the side, keeping it at the same level. Don't follow the cross as you move the paper. Now move the paper slowly from side to side and notice there will be a point where the cross will disappear in your vision.

The cross hasn't mysteriously vanished. What has happened is that this is the point in the eye called the optic nerve where there are no photoreceptors to convert the light waves that are coming into your eye into an image. As there are no photoreceptors, we should see a circular black dot. However we don't see a black dot, we see the cross vanishing and the page looking white.

What has happened? The brain interprets what it thinks should be there and fills in the gap in the missing vision created by the lack of photoreceptors. The brain interprets this gap as white to blend into the surroundings. We're not seeing reality, we are seeing the brain's best guesstimate. What else may be perceived as being real that isn't? Perceptions of it being difficult to talk to people?

CHAPTER 7

Inside Out

We have just covered how the brain constructs our reality. However, it gets more complicated than that. We have our external reality, but we also have our internal reality, which houses our imagination and memories. Most of us are aware of our external reality, but many of us are less aware of our inner world, and this is where our fears and limiting beliefs come from.

THE INNER WORLD

When we are creating our external reality, we are laying down a map that is specific to us based on the sensory data that is coming in and which has been filtered through our primary senses. We don't notice everything and are only aware of a small part of what is going on.

As you read this book, you may find that your mind occasionally wanders, and this is perfectly normal. You may have other thoughts that come into your mind. As you think about those thoughts, many people construct an internal picture. Some of these thoughts may be random and some may be related to the material that you're reading in this book.

You may recall an event that you associate with this book, or it may be something personal to you. The more vivid the description then the more accurate the imagined picture will be. The brain uses association. You may hear a particular song and are immediately transported back to a particular memory. Advertisers are aware of the power of association. When we see a picture of ice cream, we often want ice cream. This is called "priming".

We access our internal world as we imagine or remember things that we have to do. This is important to realise because when we speak to people and they are in their internal world, then they are not paying attention to what we are is saying. When people are accessing their internal world, they are technically in a trance state. This is a perfectly normal occurrence, and we constantly flip between the external world and the internal world in a series of mini trances. Has anyone ever spoken to you and you didn't hear them? Someone may have spoken, but the junction box in your brain did not bring it to consciousness as you were thinking about something else.

Let's have a look now at how we lay down our memories. For this, we are going to enter the world of NLP or neurolinguistic programming which can be thought of as software for the mind.

Lay It Down

We lay down our memories from interpreting the data that comes in through our five senses. These senses are sight, sound, taste, smell and feel. We can add to those senses by including a feeling that we had when we laid down the memory. This is difficult to explain. Some people describe this as a summer feeling or a Christmas feeling or a particular childhood memory feeling. Think about how you feel when you hear a song that reminds you of a particular event in your childhood. If the song is important enough, we often get the accompanying feelings we had at the time we created the memory.

All memories are a lie. You are recalling the data that was received through your senses to encode that memory and it is only an interpretation of the events this took place. Have you ever had a situation where you have watched a sports game and you have been supporting a particular team that won? All the reporting after the game and the consensus was that your team completely dominated and deserved to win. You then speak to somebody who supported the opposing team. You listen in sheer disbelief as they describe how their team was robbed of a victory. We may wonder are they referring to the same game.

Have you ever seen a film for the second time and spotted things that you missed first time around? Another example would be when you're with a friend who relays a story common to both of you to a third party. As you listen to the story, thoughts of "this is not quite how I remember the story" come to mind.

Although we process information through our five senses, we all have a preferred sense that we will use to recall memories. For example, for some, it may be a feeling, for others they may recall an image or a sound. This does not mean that we will always recall a memory using just one particular sense, but there is often one that we prefer.

Representational Systems

Visual - Images
Auditory - Sounds
Auditory Digital - Talking to ourselves
Kinaesthetic - Feelings
Olfactory - Smell
Gustatory - Taste

While we use all of these representational systems at different times, most of us have a preferred or dominant system, which is known as the "lead representational system". This is not a conscious choice, and it takes place at an unconscious level. The breakdown in representational systems as an approximate is,

Visual - 40% of the population
Kinaesthetic - 40% of the population
Auditory - 20% of the population.
Gustatory and Olfactory represent a low percentage.

Whether it is exactly a 40/40/20 split is not important. It is true enough to be true. The main two lead systems that I have found the most useful to identify are visual and kinaesthetic. Therefore, we need to sharpen our awareness to establish this. The big challenge is that we are fighting against our limited attention capabilities.

The same data coming into the brain is interpreted differently by us all. Too cold for one person is just right for another.

Where is the Map?

With this information, people construct their map of the world. No two maps look identical. Each one of us has our map, and this is determined by an interpretation of data coming into the brain through the five senses which are visual, auditory, kinaesthetic, olfactory and gustatory (VAKOG). In the world of NLP neurolinguistic programming (software for the brain) there is a phrase that says that "the map is not the territory". It is key to understand this, and it explains why nobody thinks that they are being awkward, weird or difficult.

When we are communicating or presenting to people or speaking, it's not our map of the world that matters, but it is theirs. It is always amusing to listen to two politicians of different political persuasions arguing. They are both correct based on their maps of the world!

Project Recall

People recall their maps of the world differently. Let's use an example to illustrate this. Suppose that I was to ask you to think about your favourite holiday and ask you to describe it to me. For many, they would simply recall an image and then describe it. However, do you recall the image as if you are in the experience and seeing it through your eyes, which is called an associated state, or are you looking at yourself in the image as if watching it in a movie theatre? The latter is called a disassociated state. We have stronger emotions with an associated state than we do with a disassociated state.

There is a lot more to recalling the image than just seeing it through your own eyes or seeing it as if at the movie theatre. Is the image moving or is it stationary? Is it in colour or is it in black and white? How sharp is the image? Is it blurry or sharply in focus? If I was to ask you to draw a frame around the image with your hands, how big would it be? These variables represent

49

submodalities and we can change those and in doing so, we can change the experience and our emotional attachment to it.

Let's experiment with this now. I want you to recall again your favourite holiday. Experience it as if being there and recall the memory as if seeing it through your own eyes. Now recall any smells, tastes or sounds associated with the image and recall any feelings that you may have had at that time. Next, if the image was in black and white, make it in colour and if it was stationary to make it move. Make it sharper and brighter. Now expand the image like you would if you were expanding an image on an electronic device such as a phone or tablet and make it as big as an IMAX screen. Now notice how you feel.

We're now going to do the reverse. Take the image that you've recalled and make it stationary, black and white, duller and less sharp. Now step out of the image and imagine that you are now sitting in a movie theatre watching the stationary black and white image. Make the image smaller and smaller and shrink it to the size of a postage stamp and push it out into the distance. Take a moment to notice how you feel. Many people don't like this feeling and want the original image and feeling back. When the image is shrunk, the corresponding emotions shrink with it too. You can play around with this and notice how your emotions change.

The point of this exercise is to show you that everybody has a strategy for laying down and recalling memories. It is important to realise the difference between an associated state which is seeing something through your own eyes and the disassociated state which is seeing something as if you're in the movie theatre.

Let's look at some examples. People who are smokers are usually very good at disassociating themselves from any potential harm that they may be doing themselves.

People who suffer from depression are very good at using their imagination in the associated state as they experience it as if seeing through their own eyes. What internal pictures do you make when thinking about talking to anybody or when communicating?

We can do a similar thing with the internal voice. What does your internal voice sound like? Where is it? Point to where you hear it. Is it serious, fun or commanding? Is it loud or quiet? We can do a similar exercise with our internal voice. We can change the volume, pace, timbre and emotion of it and we can move it to a new location. We can change it to a silly voice and move its location. Try this and notice how you feel.

CHAPTER 8

Don't Stop Believing

The author discussed in depth in the book "Inside the Mind of Sales" the importance of belief and how it affects the outcome. Let's look at belief. Belief is the first step in the process of any form of communication. Henry Ford famously said:

"Whether you think that you can or think that you can't, you're right?"

Let's explore the science behind "belief" and see if thoughts really can affect the outcome. The English astronomer Arthur Eddington summarised it nicely when he said that the universe is not only stranger than we imagine, but it is stranger than we could imagine. There has been research carried out in the field of quantum mechanics, which is physics at the micro-level, of how the impact of thoughts affects the outcome. Let's go ahead and explore weird worlds.

Welcome to Weird Worlds

Helmut Schmidt investigated whether thoughts could affect the outcome back in the 1970s and devised an experiment. The experiment was quite extraordinary in terms of what it showed.

Schmidt set up a random event generator to provide independent random results. A random event generator was connected to two light bulbs. There was a red light and a green light. A radioactive isotope was connected to ensure that the results were truly random and to ensure that red lights were shown fifty per cent of the time and green lights were shown fifty per cent of the time.

Volunteers were asked to see if they could alter the number of one particular colour of light being shown. The results were analysed and the volunteers had managed to alter the proportion of one light over the other. The results were regarded as statistically significant.

Many people were sceptical of Schmidt and thought that he had perhaps rigged the equipment. However, this experiment has been replicated twenty nine times, including by members of the Sceptic Society! Every time it has been carried out, there is always a statistically significant result. It seems like we really can alter events through our belief system. Let's explore further how belief can affect the outcome.

Plant Talk

Cleve Backster was a former CIA lie detector specialist with an excellent reputation and was heavily involved with scientific research in the polygraph community. In the late 1950s, he developed the Backster Zone Comparison test. This technique is still used by government agencies and the military for reading polygraphs.

In February 1966 he had been working all night in the laboratory and he decided to water a plant, a Dracaena Fragrans that his secretary had brought in to brighten up his office. Backster had just watered the dracaena plant and wondered if his polygraph equipment could measure the rate at which the water rose from the root into the leaf. In humans, the polygraph can measure the change in electrical resistance between two different locations on the skin. The theory is that people sweat when they lie, and sweat decreases electrical resistance. The electrodes from Backster's lie detector test were attached to each side of one of the dracaena's leaves. He expected to see the polygraph's recording chart trend upward as the leaf's moisture content increased.

However, the tracing gradually trended downward, which was unexpected. Then, about one minute into the tracing, a puzzling mountain shape was drawn on the recording paper by the pen. This peak closely resembled the tracings associated with emotional stimulation in humans. This was puzzling. How could Backster test this and see if the plant felt threatened? At that moment, Backster had a thought. What if he were to burn the plant? The moment that he had the thought of burning the plant, the pen recording the trace became very active and started quivering violently. The plant had reacted to the thought!

Backster named this phenomenon "primary perception" and he published a book titled "The Secret Life of Plants" in 1973. His research suggested that there was a basic form of communication taking place amongst life, from single cell bacteria to the cells that make up larger organisms. This communication between cells and emotions can take place over 100 miles away!

One theory that may help us understand this is known as non-locality. Experiments have shown that when researchers change the polarity of one photon (small particle of light) the polarity of the corresponding photon or packet of light changes too. This change takes place faster than the speed of light. Einstein predicted that travelling faster than the speed of light is impossible, yet this is what we appear to be observing. This is known as quantum entanglement, or as Einstein called it, "spooky at a distance".

Reception to Backster's Experiment

Backster had many critics. Many could not replicate the experiment. However, they had failed to realise the effect of the observer effect (the act of observation affects the outcome). This is now well documented and without question. Backster discovered that when experimenting, you cannot look at the output from the plant as the act of observation blocks the response. Others have replicated his results and these include the Russian scientist Alexander Dubrov and Marcel Vogel, who was at IBM at the time of his studies.

Implications for Communication

These experiments have potentially profound effects on our communication. This shows the importance of state control and of controlling our thoughts. From my experience, I cannot tell you how many times I have wished that a particular event could be moved or cancelled and then I receive an email or a phone call asking if it would be possible to rearrange.

"Be careful what you wish for. It might just come true!"

CHAPTER 9

Rules of the Human Game

I n this chapter, we are going to look at how people think. There are several biases that we all have. Everyone is different, but *"just not that different"*. This is good news for us.

Which Radio Station Are You Tuned To?

Let's start with our first principle. Everybody is tuned to radio station WIIFM. In other words, "What's in it for me?" If the conversation does not convey any benefit or is of no interest to the other person, then it's unlikely to have any impact.

Looking Out For Number One

When looking at a group photograph of us and our friends or family, who do we look at first? Yes, we all know who it is. Even the most altruistic or unselfish people always look at themselves first before looking at others. You may say that you know someone who does a lot of voluntary work or gives to charity. While this is highly commendable, the act of doing this makes some people feel good. People always do things for a reason which is not always obvious, but behind it is usually an emotion and often a strong one.

Resistance

People will resist in four different scenarios.

1. What other people think about them
2. What they think about themselves
3. What they believe to be true
4. What you tell them and accept what they conclude

The "F You" Principle

If I were to push or pull you, there would be a natural physical resistance to this. There is a similar principle at work when verbally telling or forcing someone. It's what I call the "F You" principle. Even though you know the person is correct, there is a part of you going "F you!" Somebody may be forced into a decision by an authority figure or a boss but this is likely to be short lived and only when under their control or supervision. They will comply but don't want to do it.

No One likes to be Proved Wrong

Even though people know that they're wrong, no one likes admitting it and will hold on to any form of evidence or belief no matter how esoteric to back up the fact that they're right. A better approach is to allow them to hold on to their belief system no matter how bizarre it may seem to you. No one likes a smart arse (smart ass).

Have you ever had a situation where you've been involved in a discussion and it gets heated? The discussion may be about a topic with which you didn't feel particularly strongly about, to begin with. Then, as somebody tries to force their opinion upon you and prove that you are wrong, the more they force, the more you defend your position. At the end of the discussion, you may have thought I didn't feel that strongly in the first place! It's the fact that somebody tried to prove you wrong that brought out your basic protection mechanism. Your emotional brain was triggered.

If somebody has managed to prove you wrong, think about how you feel. Do you thank them or do you have a feeling of resentment towards them? You may even store this away and want to even the score in the future. Such is the power of the emotional brain.

Everyone Likes To Be Liked

Everybody likes to be liked and appreciated. Some people will pretend as if it does not bother them. Just watch the reaction from someone as they get defensive if you criticise them.

"Sticks and stones may break my bones but words will never hurt me"

This is an expression however, words are very powerful, as we shall see later in this book.

Criteria and Values Rule

We have learned that everybody has their map of the world. From our life experiences, we lay down our criteria and values. These are things we look for that are important to us and represent our value set. For example, some people may place the success of their business as a key priority, whereas others may place the family as the most important aspect.

Many of our beliefs are laid down very early in life. If we look at babies, they are predominantly in the delta brain wave state if brain waves are measured. These are the same brain waves emitted when we are sleeping.

Between the ages of two and seven, the brain is predominantly in the theta state, which is a highly suggestible state. The brain emits these waves when in the hypnagogic, deep hypnotic trance or deep meditative state. This is when many of our fundamental beliefs are laid down without critical analysis.

Between the ages of seven and eleven, the brain is predominantly in the alpha wave state. The brain emits alpha waves when daydreaming or light trance state. This is also associated with a suggestible state.

Whenever you are speaking to somebody, it is advisable to stay within their criteria and values and make sure that the conversation does not conflict with these criteria and values. Remember that for something to be perceived as true, it does not have to be true, it just has to be plausible.

People Prefer a Comfortable Lie

People prefer a comfortable lie to an uncomfortable truth. Imagine that you hold a certain belief set that is false. Someone then questions you on this belief set and, through providing evidence, it becomes apparent that your belief set may be incorrect. Eventually, you come to a point where you realise that your belief set may be wrong. You now have a choice. Discount the new information, continue with the belief set and accept the comfortable lie, or accept the new information and accept that your belief set was incorrect and have a belief set.

People dislike admitting that they are wrong and will hold on to pre-existing beliefs. It's easier to fool someone than to convince them they have been fooled. It is very difficult to get somebody to think in a new way. I heard a great phrase once that said:

> *"I have given up trying to change the world. Half the world doesn't want to know and the other half doesn't care."*

This is a very important principle to remember. You are very unlikely to change somebody's criteria and values. Wars have been fought over religion, such is the passion to defend a belief set. It is better to allow the person to continue their belief system even if this is incorrect and allow them to save face. Unless, of course, you want to alienate them. Remember, everybody's map is accurate to them.

When Do We Say No

1. The suspicious mind always says no
2. The confused mind always says no
3. The angry mind always says no

Most of us don't intend to make people angry or suspicious, however, many of us confuse people and unintentionally annoy them. With this comes resistance. Many of us have had the experience of listening to someone and thinking:

> *"What are earth are they on about? I can't understand a word!"*

You may even have had stronger thoughts!

Where's Grandma?

A great tip I received years ago, particularly when communicating something technical or that involves specialist knowledge is:

> *"If your Grandma can't understand it, then it is too complicated!"*

Learning to Trade

When presenting something, we must make sure that the reptilian and limbic brains are interested and not threatened or confused. This short story illustrates how important it is to make sure that if presenting that people don't feel threatened but follow and understand exactly what you are saying.

I saw an advert for a free training session showing how to trade in currency to be held at one of the local hotels. With my background in Investment Management, I decided to attend the event to find out a bit more about currency trading and to see how the event was being run.

I arrived at the hotel, parked my car outside, and entered the main room, where there were about twenty people seated. The presentation started, and we were shown an introductory video. The video was professionally shot and showed the expertise and credibility of the company, together with the currency trading system.

After the video had finished, the presenter, a well-educated man in his early thirties, explained that he was going to demystify currency trading and was going to demonstrate a live trade during the presentation. I realised that there would be a sales pitch and upsell at the end, but I was curious to see how the pitch was going to be presented. He began by making things very simple and explained some basics of currency trading. Then, as things progressed, it gradually became a bit more technical. At one point, he used a graph to illustrate a point, but my attention momentarily had wandered. The point was critical to understanding the trading strategy, and I felt slightly uneasy, as I was now not following what he was saying. I could feel the frustration building. To reduce frustration and seek clarity, I did what many of us would do. I put my hand up to ask a question. My reptilian brain had kicked in. I was confused.

Then something bizarre happened. The presenter dismissively, while pointing at me with the back of his hand, stated that he was not taking questions. I had driven to the venue, spent money on parking and I thought it perfectly reasonable to be want to understand the presentation. I now could not follow what was going on and was beginning to feel even more uneasy. I raised my hand again. The presenter then rather rudely said, *"Look, I'm not taking questions!"* and I said to him, *"Well, if you are not going to take any questions, how am I supposed to follow what you are talking about?"* He then repeated, *"I am not taking questions!"*

Confusion had now turned to annoyance. I was now acting from my reptile and midbrain and did something completely illogical. After being in the presentation for only ten minutes, I closed my book and got up and left with the internal voice in my head saying, *"I'm not listening to another word of this, this is complete nonsense!"*

On arrival back home and having had time to reflect and critically evaluate what had happened, I realised that leaving early was not the wisest thing to have done. I had missed out on both learnings and the formula for the event. My reptile brain had kicked in and together with it, my midbrain. My critical brain had not had the chance to analyse whether my actions were logical. The reptile brain had caused a shutdown in my critical thinking and created the fight or flight response. I simply had to leave the room. This story just goes to show you how we can all act irrationally, and even though I understand how the brain works, I was still at its mercy.

If we put this in the context of a conversation, if we confuse people, then we are likely to experience a shutdown in their thinking. This is before they even get to evaluate your proposition. The confused mind always says no and the suspicious mind always says no. In this particular story, the confused mind said *"No, and let's get out of here!"*

People Respond to a Reason

Experiments by Ellen Langer, the Harvard social psychologist, showed that we will achieve a more successful outcome when asking for a favour if we provide a reason. Langer asked people who were waiting in a queue or a line to use the library photocopying machine a small favour. When Ellen used the phrase:

"Excuse me, I have five pages to photocopy. May I use the Xerox machine because I'm in a rush?"

And ninety four per cent allowed her to skip ahead of them in the queue or line compared with only sixty per cent when she omitted the phrase:

"Because I'm in a rush"

She then tried a third phrase, where she substituted:

"Because I have five pages" in place of *"because I'm in a rush."*

This time ninety three per cent agreed. The key point in this experiment was not the actual reason given, but the use of the word "because". For something to be perceived as true, it doesn't have to be true, it just has to be plausible. Get into the habit of using the word because when want somebody to do something and just notice the difference in the outcome.

The Seesaw of Reciprocity

The law of reciprocity is a hard-wired behavioural bias. In short, it means that, if somebody does something for us, we usually like to return the favour. If you've ever been invited around for dinner by some friends, you may casually mention that they must come round to yours next time. However, let's assume before you have time to invite them around that they invite you around for lunch. Now, you realise that they've invited you around twice and you haven't reciprocated. The seesaw is out of balance and it feels uncomfortable. Your friends then invite you around for drinks. You either decline because you feel too embarrassed or insist on them coming around to yours. There will be some people who will take advantage, but for most of us, we want to make sure that the seesaw goes to level again. The law of reciprocity can be used very effectively to gain power and compliance. It often produces a "yes" response to a request because of a feeling of indebtedness.

Following the herd

The law of social proofing. Thinking is hard work and, where possible, humans often outsource their thinking to others. We use this to make a perceived correct decision based on what others deem is correct. Usually, when many people do something, it is perceived as the right thing to do. Bar staff or bartenders and café owners will often put money in a jar to give the impression that tipping is normal behaviour, as will the street musician with coins in his guitar case. Nightclubs will often deliberately have a small queue or line to give the impression of popularity. Have you ever wandered past two restaurants and one is busy and the other one is quiet? Which one would you choose? We are all wired similarly!

We Like People Just Like Us

We prefer to say yes to the requests of someone we know and like. Both researchers and compliance professionals know the importance of similarity. We like people who are similar to us. This is true for opinions, personality traits, background, hobbies or life-style. Therefore, the more alike you are to somebody then the more they will like you. This is largely an unconscious response. Dressing similarly is one way and emphasising similar backgrounds, hobbies and interests is another. We are more likely to support our sex, culture and country. We will support people that represent us and that are like us.

Deference to Authority

Human beings are hard-wired to have a deference to authority and perceived or real authority figures. People in power are aware of this and exaggerate this using uniforms, clothing and titles. This deference to authority not only applies to people in senior positions but also to those who are deemed, experts. One of the ways that you can convey this expertise is through recognised uniforms. This is why doctors wear white coats and why judges and the clergy wear robes. This principle is so important that it can be illustrated in the experiment conducted by Stanley Milgram, a Yale University Psychologist, back in 1953. The experiment tested obedience to authority. It measured the willingness of men from a diverse range of occupations with varying levels of education, to obey an authority figure. The authority figure wearing a lab coat and holding a clipboard instructed them to perform acts that conflicted with their conscience. They led participants to believe that they were assisting an unrelated experiment, in which they had to administer electric shocks to a "learner". An actor played the learner. Every time the learner got a question wrong, the volunteers were told to administer electric shock. This increased in intensity every time the learner answered a question incorrectly. The actor would scream in pain. While the shocks were fake, the participants were told that they were real. These fake electric shocks were gradually increased to levels that would have been fatal. The experiment found, unexpectedly, that a very high proportion of subjects would fully obey the instructions, even though they knew that the doses of electricity being administered, albeit reluctantly, were fatal.

Politicians know that to change people's reality, then you must change people's perceptions. You may have noticed that when the president of the United States or the Prime Minister of Great Britain wants to deliver an important message, they do so wearing an expensive suit and a tie. It is delivered from behind a lectern with flags in the background and a carefully constructed set.

Now let's change things a bit. Let's remove the set, the flags and the lecterns. Now imagine these leaders were to deliver their message wearing flip-flops, shorts and the latest Iron Maiden T-shirt. How much authority do they convey now?

The message now has a very different tone. Have you ever met someone dressed in shorts and a t-shirt when you are used to seeing them in business attire? The perception changes. People say that you shouldn't judge a book by its cover. However, the cover is all we have until we open the book. Perception is important to remember when speaking to people. It's not just how you look, but how you sound and act that is important, too. It's not what you say, but how you say it. As the late Frank Carson, an Irish comedian, said, "It's the way I tell em!"

Loss Aversion

Loss plays a big part in people's thinking and actions. People are more motivated by the thought of losing something than by the thought of gaining something of equal value. For example, if homeowners are told how much money they could lose from inadequate insulation, they are more likely to insulate their homes than those who are told how much money they could save. I remember I once put my card into the bank cash dispenser and walked away. I can still remember that memory vividly as it was a loss as opposed to when I won something when I was at the horse racing for the day.

Scarcity Principle

This is a powerful principle and is used in marketing because it works. When something becomes scarce, we want it because of the fear of missing out. If you are selling something and you mention that there is a limited supply or that there are only three left, people will act quickly and not procrastinate. We see this used everywhere from online marketers, booking services etc. and when people construct offers. Sometimes we see this as a deadline tactic, such as the sale ends tomorrow or as a countdown timer. If you need people to take action, imply scarcity.

People Want What They Can't Have

Have you ever thought about wanting something and then the moment that you find you can't have it, the desire to have it increases? I remember being in a café and spotting a cake that I was considering buying. Then thought I wouldn't bother. The woman in front of me bought the cake and the little voice inside my head said:

"I can't believe this. I was going to have that cake!"

Next time you want someone to come to your party, say:

"I have a party this weekend. You are welcome to come but I'm not sure it's your thing. I don't think you will enjoy it"

They will be there!

Too Successful?

It's nice to mention some success that you have had, but not too many. This goes for being overly positive. Many people will be pleased for you, but there is a part of them that will identify parts of their life that are not perfect and they may be envious. Admitting to minor flaws without complaining gains credibility. I know one person who continually goes on about how successful he is and then complains that he has no friends. I wonder why?

CHAPTER 10

Different People, Different Approach

Recently, I was delivering a talk on advanced communication skills. The subject of body language came up. One attendee asked if body language varies between different personalities. I thought this was a great question because indeed it does. You can learn a lot about somebody, and their personality type, just by looking at their body language and nonverbal communication. Let's look at some personality types.

PERSONALITY TYPES

Personality types have been around for a long time. Hippocrates called these the four temperaments. He established the four archetypes of people's personalities. This has evolved. More recently, Myers-Briggs, as an adaptation of the theory of psychological types, produced by Carl Gustav Jung, has produced 16 personality types. This relies on filling in a questionnaire to identify the different types. While this information is useful, it is just not practical to give a questionnaire to someone and then ask them to fill it in. We need a method where we can use our observational and awareness skills instead. This is where our understanding of body language and nonverbal communication will serve us well.

IDENTIFYING A PERSONALITY

My favoured method is the Merrill-Wilson model. It is simple to understand and fast to identify. The four personality types are Dominant, Expressive, Amiable, and Analytical. There are two main variables to identify a personality type. Are they better with either facts & data or relationships? Are they introverted (low assertion) or extroverted (high assertion)?

From this, we get four main types as shown in Fig.3:

Dominant
Fact-Based, Extrovert, High Emotional Control
Analytical
Fact-Based, Introvert, High Emotional Control
Amiable
Relationship-Based, Introvert, Low Emotional Control
Expressive
Relationship-Based, Extrovert, Low Emotional Control

People will move between these boxes in different situations and can be any of the four, but will feel more comfortable in one. The archetype that people fall into is easy to recognise once we know what to look for. This can be useful when dealing with people. It can give you an indication when communicating with them and selecting which type of strategy to adopt.

The Clues

The first step is to identify whether somebody is an introvert or an extrovert. Having done that, then pay attention to the warmth of the greeting that you get. This will give you an indication of whether emotional thinking will influence decisions or not.

Dominant - Aim to be in control

Dominant people exhibit control and power. They often display a firm handshake, direct eye contact and controlled body language with little blinking of the eyes. Expect to see strong eye contact that can sometimes be a little uncomfortable. They will often use the dominant handshake where the knuckles are facing upwards and the palm faces downward. The body language reflects control and dominance and they don't move much. When they move, it is with purpose. They often place their hands on their hips to make themselves bigger. Body positions include standing upright to appear taller with their head back. Sometimes they may sit with their hands behind their head in an outstretched position. These people often like to play power games, which will include having a larger desk or being more elevated than the person with whom they are meeting. To demonstrate control, they may swivel the chair to the side or even with their back facing you. This all illustrates the power and control that they perceive they have.

Early in my sales career, I remember visiting a dominant in his office. He took the whole control aspect a stage further. I was young at the time and was fazed by his behaviour. Not only did he swivel his seat around with his back facing me, but he also did so while eating a bacon roll (a loose equivalent to a bagel if you are from the US). This was beyond dominance. It was rude.

I was young, and didn't have the confidence to pull him up on it. At parties, dominants like to make an impressive entrance. They tend not to smile, as this is perceived as a sign of weakness. When they laugh in public, it is in a very controlled way. They like other people to come up to them. They are often in the centre of the room, surrounded by people of lower status. The people of lower status will exhibit lower status non-verbal signals, such as lowering of the head.

Expressive - Aim to be noticed

Expressives often greet people with a warm greeting and display an enthusiastic handshake. They are less formal. They are friendly and warm but are not afraid to say no. They have less control over their body language and it is very expressive. They are animated when they speak. Expect to see palm gestures as they use their arms and hands to communicate their excitement. There is often a higher degree of lower body movement. Expressives move a lot and tend to blink a lot, too. Decisions are based on emotion. Expect to see a lot of comfortable eye contact. They are not overbearing and eye contact moves around a lot. When seated, expressives will often take up a lot of space and often in some unusual seated positions. As their attention span is very low, they are easily distracted and display signs of distraction. Expressives enjoy things that are exciting and new. Expect to see displays of boredom or disinterest if they don't agree with you. They smile a lot and are not afraid to laugh. At parties, expressives are usually the centre of attention and at the hub of what is going on. They like to make a grand entrance acknowledging everyone as they come into the room.

Amiable - Aim to blend in

Amiables are introverts. They aim to please and dislike confrontation and will often see both sides of the argument. They will often greet with a soft handshake. They are trusting and want everyone to get along. Their body language reflects being introverted, and they tend to make themselves smaller and less conspicuous. They do this by keeping their arms and legs under control and close to the body. They are literally making themselves less noticeable. Their head is often down in a slightly lowered position to avoid being noticed. Amiables hate confrontation and do not display strong eye contact. They don't like confrontation or being pressurised. Signs of discomfort are often displayed if pressure is applied to them. They tend to move slower and with controlled movement. At parties, amiables are often at the side of the room. This ties in with not wanting to be noticed. They are often involved in a conversation not with a group of people but with another person on a one-to-one basis. When they smile, it is more of a warm smile and when they laugh, it is more controlled. When an amiable enters the room, they aim to do so without being noticed.

Analytical - Aim to work things out

Analyticals love data, details and spreadsheets. They often walk with their head leaning forwards. These people are introverted and very often have very low external awareness. They have very poor eye contact and tend to look down a lot when they speak to you. They have a high degree of emotional control and can give the impression that they are not interested in what somebody else is saying. This comes from their lack of understanding of how to engage. As they have low self-awareness skills, they will sometimes wear some unusual clothes that don't quite fit in with the occasion. Their low awareness skills can also be observed with their lack of facial expressions that reflect the different emotions in a story that someone may be telling. They tend not to smile a lot. This can give the impression of being aloof and unengaged. Fig. 3 summarises the different personality types.

Changing Styles

Using this analysis of body language enables us to adapt our style when engaging with other people. If, for example, we meet an amiable, we would know that we would need to adapt our style. They enjoy reassurance and like things at a slow pace. Trust is very important to them. If you are dealing with an expressive ask them about their holiday expect and them to talk a lot. They will be very open with information and will be more than happy to talk enthusiastically and expressively. If you are dealing with a dominant, expect to keep the relationship professional and to get to the point fairly quickly. Dominants like to challenge people. Expect to be challenged and to know everything about your subject. If you are dealing with an analytical, expect to find it difficult to have much of a conversation with them. Everything is based on logic and process. They would expect you to explain what you are doing and to know all the technical details, including all the micro details, if you are asked. These people dislike generalisation and disorganisation. Expect them to turn up on time. They will expect you to turn up on time, too.

Type	Strengths	Weaknesses
Dominant	Determined Decisive Independent	Lack of Empathy Impatient Domineering
Expressive	Communication Enthusiastic Creative	Disorganised Talkative Unfinished work
Amiable	Diplomatic Supportive Loyal	Not assertive Reactive Change resistant
Analytical	Thorough Disciplined Structured	Rigid Unemotional Perfectionist

Fig.3

CHAPTER 11

Rapport Building

R apport is a deep level of communication and understanding between two or more people. It is fundamental to any relationship. With rapport, just about anything is possible and without it, very little. Before looking at rapport building, let's examine the science behind rapport.

Looking in the Mirror

Mirror neurones were discovered by researchers Giacomo Rizzolatti and Vittorio Gallese at the University of Palma in Italy. They were studying activity in monkey brains. They found it did not matter whether an action was carried out or was observed by a monkey, it was the same regions of the monkey's brain that was activated. This led to the concept of the mirror neurone. Similar results were observed when looking at the brains of humans. The mirror neurone is a bit of a misnomer. Today, it is agreed that there is no such single neuron at work, but a network of neurons working together. The more attention that we give to an observation, then the more likely we are to copy the behaviour. We see this when we meet people who have different accents. Our speech and accent change accordingly to enable us to fit in better. It has also been shown that the more we imitate other people, then the more we like them and the more they like us.

Dr Ulf Dimberg from Sweden in 2000, carried out an experiment where he showed volunteers frowning, smiling and with expressionless faces. Even if trying to control our emotions and expressions in every case, minute expressions occurred. This showed that mirroring was the natural tendency.

The ability to sense what other people are feeling is an important factor in allowing us to connect, or communicate effectively with them. The smoothness of this interaction depends to a great extent on the establishment of entrainment or a connection between individuals.

BUILDING RAPPORT

To influence someone, we first have to have rapport. It is the magic ingredient. With it, just about anything is possible and without it, very little. Once we have rapport, we can then look at influencing people. When people are in rapport, they often say "we are on the same wavelength". This expression is an excellent metaphor for considering rapport and there is support for this from the research.

Being at the Seaside

Think about being at the beach or by the sea and consider two waves interacting with each other. If two waves are in sync with each other, then you have constructive interference and the wave becomes larger. In rapport terms, this represents a strengthening of the relationship. If, however, the waves are not in sync, then the peaks and troughs cancel each other out and you have destructive interference. In terms of rapport, this means a destruction of the relationship or no rapport. Using this wave analogy, the closer the two waves are to being in sync then the stronger will be the resultant wave. What does this mean for rapport? The more you are alike somebody then the more rapport you will have with them.

Stacking

A good analogy for this is to think of rapport as pieces of paper stacked in a pile on a table. Each component of rapport is represented by a single sheet of paper. A single sheet of paper on its own is very flimsy and is not solid. You could blow on the piece of paper and it would move. Imagine meeting somebody for the first time and you find out that they are from the same town as you. This would represent a single layer of rapport or sheet of paper in our analogy. You then find out that you went to the same school. This represents another layer or sheet of paper in our analogy. You find out that you have similar hobbies and political leanings. These additional things in common represent additional layers of rapport, just like adding more sheets of paper to the pile. The more sheets you add to the pile, the stronger it becomes. This is the same with rapport and I call this layering. Just as the pile gets stronger, then so does the level of rapport. Birds of a feather do flock together. I like to consider five types of rapport.

1. Content Rapport
2. Physical Rapport
3. Secret Rapport
4. Timing Rapport
5. Unusual Rapport

Content Rapport

Content rapport includes things that we have in common. This includes interests, background, home town, life experiences, etc. Here we are looking to become as alike to another person as we can. In discussions, we are looking for areas of commonality and not areas of difference. Look for areas of similarity such as music, hobbies, place of origin, films, sport, and food. A useful tip is if you can discover and share an unusual interest, then this builds massive rapport. For example, if you collect beer cans, or collect corks and someone has the same interest as you, this will build massive rapport.

Always avoid areas of contention. For example, if you discover the person has a political persuasion that is not in line with yours, avoid that subject and change it. Focus on what you have in common, look for more, and avoid what you don't have in common. We must use correct questioning techniques to elicit this information. These are expanded upon in the section on questioning.

Physical Rapport

With physical rapport, we are looking to be as similar to other people as we can in how they move, speak, and look. There are a lot of factors at play when trying to build physical rapport, and a method that makes this easier would be useful.

There are two methods. One is unconscious and the other one is a conscious approach.

Physical Mirroring

One of the fastest ways to build rapport with somebody is to adopt a similar body language. People who are in rapport have similar body language to each other. We can witness this in social situations and by observing people in restaurants, bars, and cafes. It's like a dance and is done at an unconscious level.

Once aware of this, you will notice how people lean towards each other, adopt similar body positions, and then mirror each other. When people first discover and become aware of mirroring, it is often a major revelation.

There are three methods for doing this:-

1. Mirroring
2. Matching
3. Cross matching

We will explore this in this chapter.

Going for a Walk

A natural phenomenon that often occurs when people are in rapport is that their legs synchronise when walking. You may have noticed this. We can use this phenomenon when we meet somebody and walk with them. Simply synchronising our legs with theirs as we walk develops an unconscious rapport. Using something simple like this enhances the stacking principle.

I once met a client and we weren't naturally on the same wavelength. We were meeting to explore the possibility of having an external consultant come in to help them. The client suggested we go for a coffee. As we walked to the coffee shop, I wanted to make sure that we were building rapport quickly. Simply matching my legs and synchronising them to that of the client created initial rapport and began the stacking process.

After the initial meeting, I was invited back to meet with the client's boss. At the second meeting, I wanted to build rapport quickly. I made sure to get myself into the correct state. I enhanced this with some conscious mirroring of the boss' body language. During the meeting, I noticed that not only were the boss and I mirroring each other, but that the other individual was mirroring as well. This meant that I was in rapport with both of them. As the meeting drew to a close, the boss summarised that we all seemed of a like mind.

Secret Rapport

A very powerful way to build rapport and trust with somebody is to share a secret. Sharing a secret will often cause people to lean forward as their curiosity is aroused. Reputational risk is important and telling mistruths or making things up will do your relationship and reputation no good. If there is information that you can share with somebody, this will build rapport and trust.

Timing Rapport

The best way to illustrate timing rapport is by using an example. Have you ever had a situation where you've met somebody, got on very well and said we must meet up for a coffee or a drink sometime? The other person agrees and is keen to do so. Time then moves on and the memory of that person fades and it starts to feel a little uncomfortable to get in touch. The longer we leave it, the worse it becomes. It's the same thing when it comes to dating. The next meeting must take place, fairly shortly afterwards, to continue developing the relationship.

I liken this to seeds in a garden. If we plant seeds, some of them may grow. However, we have to look after the seeds to make sure that they are not harmed by frost or eaten by the birds. We also have to make sure that the seeds receive the correct amount of water and that the correct temperature is maintained. There is quite a lot of work involved in the early stages to make sure that they survive. Then, as the seed develops into a plant, it's just the case of a bit of pruning now and again. Think about somebody you've known for many years. You don't have to see them regularly for the relationship to continue. That's because you have established deep roots with them in the first place. Another thing to be aware of is that people formulate their relationships based on common interests. As soon as those interests differ or drift apart, the relationship can break down. You may have heard of the phrase "growing apart".

Unusual Rapport

If we discover we share an unusual or specialist interest, then this will build a strong rapport. We are naturally drawn to people that share our specialist interests.

Touch Rapport

A light touch on the arm builds rapport and dramatically increases compliance. This applies to several requests including asking for money, to getting a woman's phone number. Studies have shown that touching someone on the upper arm, for just a second or two, can affect how helpful they will be. Other studies have shown that the same subtle touch significantly increases the likelihood that people leave a tip for waiters and waitresses.

It has the effect of increasing participation in supermarket taste tests, causing people to drink more in a bar, and getting people to become involved in charity work.

American researchers in one experiment approached people in the street and asked them for a dime. Touching them briefly on the upper arm increased the likelihood of getting the money by twenty per cent. This also has the effect of increasing the likelihood that people will sign petitions. In nightclubs, women accepted the offer of a dance over fifty per cent of the time after even the briefest of touches on the arm. The doubling of chance also occurred when asking for phone numbers by researchers in the street. It is important to mention that this is a brief touch and not a grab!

PACING AND LEADING

Pacing

Pacing and leading come from the world of hypnosis and NLP (neural linguistic programming) which is software for the mind. We can use this principle when using nonverbal communication. Pacing means pacing what a person is doing or pacing the experience. People like people who are like them. We can reflect this through pacing. This sets up a biofeedback loop. We can, however, go even deeper and use pacing in other areas of nonverbal communication too.

Leading

Once we have paced somebody and started mirroring them for a while, we can change our body position and notice if the other person follows us. We can then change what we are doing and see if they follow. If the person follows, you now have the phenomenon of leading. Leading is a good indicator that rapport has been established. If you find when you lead, the person is not following you, this means that not enough rapport has been built up. It is just a matter of going back, pacing again for longer and repeating the process.

You can observe pacing and leading when a group of people stands together. When the dominant person changes their body position, the others will often follow. Let's look at how we can pace someone using mirroring and matching.

MIRRORING & MATCHING

Mirroring and matching means copying someone. There are many ways that we can mirror and match. We can mirror and match body language, voice (tone, pace, volume, and choice of words) together with breathing and blinking. In this book, we are going to be focusing on physical and vocal mirroring.

Mirroring

Mirroring is copying somebody's body language just as if looking at ourselves in a mirror. If somebody raises their right hand, then to mirror them, we would raise our left hand. Mirroring is very common in both social and business situations when rapport is present. We can witness mirroring in social situations such as in restaurants, bars and cafes. It's like a dance done at an unconscious level. Once you are aware of this, you will notice how people lean towards each other, adopt similar body positions, and then mirror each other. When people first discover and notice mirroring, it is often a major revelation.

Matching

Matching is a form of mirroring which is done as if standing behind someone rather than facing them. When matching, if someone raises their right hand, then we would raise our right hand too. I prefer using mirroring as this occurs naturally and unconsciously, but matching works too.

A powerful method that we can use is to match somebody's blink rate. Blinking takes place largely unconsciously but can be overridden by the conscious mind. We can take advantage of this and match the blink rate to that of the other person. This is subtle and covert. It is rarely detected, but it's powerful.

Another powerful action is to mirror somebody's breathing rate. A word of caution here. If you look at somebody's chest, particularly if you are a male speaking to a female, this is likely to break any rapport that you may have developed. An easier way to do this is to watch somebody's shoulders. They will rise when someone breathes in and fall when they breathe out. An even easier method to mirror breathing is to breathe out when someone is speaking.

Cross Matching

With cross-matching, body language is matched not directly but covertly. An example would be if the other person is moving their foot up and down, then we would raise our finger up and down at the same tempo.

Vocal Mirroring

As well as physically mirroring people, we can auditorially mirror them. When people speak, many have their favourite words. These are words that are almost like a catchphrase. If you pick up on these and reflect them back, this builds rapport.

Aside from mirroring words, it is possible to mirror how people speak. Have you ever changed your accent slightly when you speak when in the company of others? If so, this is a form of mirroring. When people speak, there is the volume, pace, tone, timbre, expression, and emotion that is conveyed in the voice.

Echo Technique

The most important words that a person hears are the words that they have just said. A very powerful way to build rapport is using the "Echo Technique". This technique involves repeating back what someone has just said. You may say, "I can't do this, people will notice". On the contrary, they will not, and even if they did, you are just clarifying your understanding. Is there anything wrong with that?

Let's have a look at an example:

"I FEEL that it's time to upgrade our IT system as it's a little outdated?"

"So, you FEEL that it's time to upgrade your IT system as it's a little outdated?"

"Yes"

Let's suppose that we asked about the implications of having an outdated IT system:

"What does it mean for your business to have an outdated IT system?"

"It means that we don't have the flexibility or ability to integrate new processes."

"So you don't have the flexibility or ability to integrate new processes, and what would a new system do for the ability to grow your business?"

It's that easy. In the example, repeating back their words puts us in the "FEEL" representational system and you will build rapport as they interpret you are listening. For longer sentences, simply pick out some key sentences and echo these back and you will achieve the same effect.

Your critical mind may say: "I couldn't possibly do that!" First, try doing this with people you know to prove to yourself that it works before trying this with strangers or in business.

A Word of Caution

When people first discover mirroring and matching, they fall into two groups. The first group thinks I couldn't possibly use mirroring or matching because people are going to spot me. They feel uncomfortable and self-aware and are reluctant to do it. The second group embraces mirroring and matching quite literally. They think that they have discovered a panacea and decide to go all out and copy somebody's every move, and consequently come across as false.

Let's address these points. We already mirror other people. It is a natural process, but we are often not aware of it. If not convinced of this, simply go to a cafe. Sit down and watch people and you will notice mirroring taking place.

For much of the time, this is outwith of conscious awareness. The best way to mirror somebody is to have a genuine desire to get to know them. As you develop rapport, automatic mirroring will take place. To get the process started, the best way to practise is in a social situation to satisfy your critical mind that it works.

When I first discovered the idea of mirroring, I was sceptical and wondered if it would work. I remember being in a bar with a client and noticed that we were both leaning against the bar.

We were facing each other with our bodies slightly angled towards the bar. I spotted we were both mirroring each other, and I decided to test mirroring. I increased the angle of my body to the bar and, to my surprise, the other person not long afterwards, copied me. Wanting to test this further, I then increased the angle of the other person, copied lean and again, this. I was stunned by this. It had worked just exactly as I had been told it would.

Some people, when they discover mirroring and matching, go all out and attempt to copy somebody's every move. This can come across as creepy. We want to be acting naturally and not behaving unusually. Let's look at two methods to improve mirroring. My favourite method is method one. It is the most powerful and the easiest to incorporate into your everyday communication.

METHOD 1

The Big Secret "R+"

The most effective method in building rapport and the most natural is to develop a strong desire to get to know and build rapport with another. I call this "R+". This relies on getting into the correct state and allowing the unconscious mind to do its magic. It comprises raising your awareness and energy levels and developing an intense desire and curiosity to get to know the person. When using this method, it's not enough to be friendly and hope that rapport occurs. It involves changing your thought process and your outlook. I have found that the best way to do this is to suspend judgement and to develop a curiosity about that person. Looking for something positive that you like about another person is enough to help flip your mind into a positive state. It could just be down to liking the type of jacket or outfit that they are wearing. Then really focus on generating an intense desire to get to know the person and a liking for them.

It has surprised me one the years with my interactions with different people as to just how much knowledge people have and in somewhat unusual areas. Getting into a habit of developing a curiosity to learn from someone else is a good habit to get into. Look for similarities and discount differences. When using this method, we need to be congruent. If the intentions and the thoughts are right, then the words and all aspects of your voice, and your body language, will reflect this.

This method, in my opinion, is the most powerful as we are hacking into the limbic or emotional brain and it is done unconsciously. However, we also need to be aware of a conscious mirroring to spot when it is present and when it has broken down.

METHOD 2

Conscious Approach

When we consciously change our nonverbal and verbal communication to match that of the other person. We need to be careful because, as this is a conscious process, it can sometimes come across as clunky. The idea is to subtly copy the body language. If someone suddenly starts scratching their head, we mustn't immediately start scratching our head. If we are speaking to somebody and they change their feet position or perhaps lean back, a good rule is to wait six seconds before we change our body position to mirror or match theirs. Then move into a similar position. Cross-matching can also be used, and this is more covert. While my preferred method is method one, method two does have its merits. Method two is useful when there does not seem to be natural chemistry and the connection does not appear to be happening.

CHAPTER 12

Wakening the Awareness

A big skill to develop to assist you in speaking to anyone is to sharpen your awareness. All the best communicators have a sharpened awareness. This doesn't happen overnight but comes with practise. It is best done in small bite-size chunks. There are two parts to this,

1. Sharpening your external awareness
2. Sharpening your internal awareness

We have discovered that we can only hold between five to nine chunks of information in our conscious awareness at once. The more that we can pass over to the unconscious mind to process information then the more effective this will be. We have already discussed that the unconscious mind learns by repetition, images, emotion and stories. The accompanying audio, if played regularly for at least 30 days, will help programme your unconscious mind for success.

One of the biggest external skills worth learning is reading body language and nonverbal communication and the reader is referred to the earlier work by the author in the book <u>Body</u>

Language How to Read Any Body. As this is such a large subject, we will cover the key principles here, and it is strongly suggested that the reader studies the aforementioned book for detailed information.

PHYSIOLOGY AND PSYCHOLOGY

When people are in an emotionally charged state, their body language reflects this. The big question is, are your emotions reflected in your physical expression and is this just a one-way process? In other words, could your physical actions affect your emotions?

Amy Cuddy found that there is a strong link between feelings of power and adopting a power pose. It is not surprising that this takes place because other disciplines, such as yoga, have body positions at their core. This means that by adopting a different body posture, it is possible to generate a corresponding emotional response. You may have noticed that when somebody is depressed, they look down at the ground and make themselves smaller. Someone who has just had a winning or a victorious moment will look up, and you may see a clenching or pumping of the fists as they make themselves bigger. This is the body language of victory and success.

The key to your success in reading body language is by reading emotions and feelings that are generated and leaked.

ACTIONS SPEAK LOUDER THAN WORDS

We are now setting the foundations and practices in motion to gain an understanding of the mind. Let's now explore the principles that will unlock the secrets to understanding body language and nonverbal communication.

Seven powerful principles

1. The outer expression is a reflection of the inner thought
2. The stronger the emotion, the stronger the body language
3. People display signs of comfort or discomfort, tension or relaxation
4. People move towards things that they like and away from things that they dislike
5. Upward gestures indicate positivity, downward gestures indicate the opposite
6. People look at things that they like and look away from things that they don't
7. Stacked gestures are more powerful than isolated gestures

Let's look at these principles in more detail.

PRINCIPLE 1

"The outer expression is a reflection of inner thought."

Human beings are communication machines. We just can't not communicate. Even the act of not communicating is an act of communication. We can all read body language it's just the degree to which we can do it.

Let's take an extreme example of the principle of the outer expression reflecting the inner thought. Think about when somebody is very angry. What sort of behaviours would they typically exhibit? They would be unlikely to be smiling and they may be snarling. We may hear them shouting. We may see on their face an expression of anger and observe that the eyebrows are lowered.

In this very simple example, we know, without listening to any of the words coming out of their mouth that they are in an angry state. As the state is one of anger, then the body reflects this state. This principle is key to understanding and is worth remembering.

PRINCIPLE 2

"The stronger the emotion, the stronger the body language."

Extreme anger is easy to spot. However, there are degrees of emotions. It becomes harder to spot mild annoyance, but the signs are still there for the trained eye. These feelings and emotions are leaked from the limbic system, or chimp brain, and the reptilian brain or paleocortex. They are expressed through body language and nonverbal communication. Let's understand these in a bit more detail.

Understanding the Reptile Brain

The reptilian brain works based on:

1. Is something a threat or a danger?
2. Is something new and exciting?
3. If it is new, get to the point quickly and make it simple.

What does this mean for body language?

1. A display of feeling threatened or discomfort
2. A display of boredom or disinterest
3. A display of confusion or annoyance

Working with the reptile and the chimp

While the neocortex or critical brain focuses on critique and evaluation, the currency of the limbic system (chimp brain) and the reptilian brain is emotions and feelings.

PRINCIPLE 3

"We react either with a display of comfort or discomfort."

Displays of Comfort

Think about someone who is in a very comfortable position and think about a situation where we could observe this. They could, for example, be sunbathing on the beach in a warm, beautiful setting. Let's think about the things that we would observe to show feelings of comfort. The muscles of their body would be relaxed together with the facial muscles and the neck. These often carry a lot of tension. The arms and the hands would be relaxed too. The breathing is likely to be slower and deeper.

Displays of Discomfort

Let's think about a situation where people would exhibit feelings of discomfort. Perhaps it may be at a busy airport with lots of flight delays and cancellations. We would see the tension in the face muscles and perhaps witness some tension in the upper shoulders, neck and back. There may be some fidgeting going on, and the arms and hands exhibit movement or tension. The breathing is likely to be shallow, high in the chest and faster.

Signs of Nerves

Many processes are carried out, beneath our level of awareness automatically, by the autonomic nervous system. The autonomic nervous system regulates bodily functions such as heart rate, blood pressure, pupil dilation, body temperature, sweating, and digestion. There are only two processes that can be consciously overridden without training. One is the blink rate and the other breathing.

PRINCIPLE 4

"People move towards things that they like and away from things that they dislike."

Think about an everyday occurrence. If there is someone that we don't like, we will try to avoid them. People will avoid going to the same places. In a business environment, people will sit as far apart from each other as they can. In a networking event, they may occupy different areas of a room. On the contrary, people who like each other will sit next to each other. In body language terms, leaning or moving towards something can show a liking or interest, while the converse can apply. The phrase "I just couldn't even bear to be in the same room as him" gives us a clue.

We have space around us we feel comfortable with. Fig 4. If you get too close to someone's space, this can cause the person to move back to create a comfortable space again. I remember once being in a meeting with a client where my colleague kept getting too close. I could see him moving backwards in the room. As people get to know each other, this space decreases and is exaggerated in an intimate relationship.

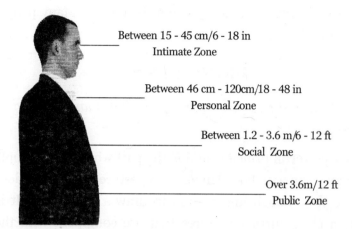

Between 15 - 45 cm/6 - 18 in
Intimate Zone

Between 46 cm - 120cm/18 - 48 in
Personal Zone

Between 1.2 - 3.6 m/6 - 12 ft
Social Zone

Over 3.6m/12 ft
Public Zone

Fig.4

PRINCIPLE 5

Upward gestures indicate positivity, downward gestures indicate the opposite.

When people are in a positive state, we see gravity defying or upward gestures. The phrase "things are looking up gives us a clue". Think about someone who is depressed. The shoulders are down. The head is down and they look down. The arms are hanging down too. Now think about a successful athlete who has just won a race. The hands and arms may be raised and they often tilt their head back and look up.

PRINCIPLE 6

"People look at things that they like and look away from things that they don't."

When we see something that we like, we look at it more often and for longer. The language again gives us a clue. "I just couldn't bear to look at her." Think about when you see something that you shouldn't or that is horrific. Many people will just look away.

PRINCIPLE 7

"Stacked gestures are more powerful than isolated gestures."

This is a powerful principle and is the part where most people have a problem with body language. A gesture in isolation does not give you enough information to draw a conclusion. It is merely a clue. Further gestures that are congruent with the original gesture will help reinforce your conclusion. The more congruent the gestures are then the more accurate your conclusion is likely to be.

Think of it a bit like if you were investigating a crime. If someone does not have an alibi does not make them guilty, but equally, it does not make them innocent!

PRACTISING AWARENESS SKILLS

We can learn to practise sharpening our internal and external awareness skills.

External Awareness Skills

Many of us, when we are going about a daily business, don't pay attention to what is going on in the external world. We may have thoughts or an internal voice that talks to us. If you want to become a better communicator, then simply become more aware. We will look at techniques that you can use to quieten the inner voice later when we look at state control. A simple technique that we can use to enhance our awareness is to look around us and describe what we are seeing. We can describe the experience using the primary senses. We can start describing the colours, sounds, smells and tastes together with the feeling that the experience is generating for us. It helps to develop a genuine curiosity about what we're seeing. When we see other people, we can try to establish as much information about them as we can. We can observe the way they walk, their body language and nonverbal cues. These are all discussed in more detail in the book Body Language How to Read Any Body by the author.

Internal Awareness Skills

Learning to sharpen our internal awareness skills takes a bit of effort as most of it takes place below our conscious level of awareness. Pay attention to any thoughts that you may have and the pictures that you may experience internally. Are you in the picture or are you watching it as if in the movie theatre? How big is the picture? Is it in focus and how far away from you is it when you're imagining it? Is it in colour and moving or stationary? Are there any sounds, smells, or tastes associated with the experience? This is the first step in sharpening internal awareness and we will explore this.

CHAPTER 13

The Power of Language

In this chapter, we're going to be looking at the power of language and how we can use it to better communicate our message and to persuade and influence people when we are speaking, presenting and communicating. It's a fascinating topic, so let's get started.

Language

Language is a system that attempts to share communal experiences. It's not that you can't articulate your experience it's just that no one else has the foundations to completely understand it. This is because it is subjective and is why miscommunication occurs.

Words have power

You can change people's perspectives and their state from the words that you choose to use. How we communicate both our reality and our map is by using words. If you can control somebody's perceptions, then you control their reality. Let's have a look at the power of words and for this, we're going to look at the research of Dr Masaru Emoto.

Dr Masaru Emoto was a Japanese scientist who revolutionised the idea that our thoughts and intentions impact the physical realm, and was one of the most important water researchers the world has known. He studied the scientific evidence of how the molecular structure in water transforms when it is exposed to human words, thoughts, sounds and intentions.

He conducted an experiment over a thirty-day period in which he placed equal amounts of cooked rice into three jars, along with an equal amount of water. He then put labels on two of the jars, indicating how they would be treated. The first jar was labelled "Thank you", and would receive positive messages. The second jar was labelled, "You idiot!" and would receive negative messages and communications. The third jar was the control and had no label.

He said "thank you" from the bottom of his heart to the "thank you" jar using an emotion of gratefulness. He yelled "You idiot" at the jar labelled "You idiot" conveying an emotion of anger and frustration. Finally, the third unlabelled rice jar was ignored conveying an emotion of indifference.

At the end of the 30th day, his observations were recorded. The jar that he thanked every day fermented spectacularly and didn't have any black mould or rotting material growing from it. The jar that he yelled and took out his anger on had turned black and was covered in mould. However, the jar that he had ignored for 30 days had even more black mould in it than the "'You idiot" rice jar. According to Dr Emoto, the rice in the jar had rotted.

With his findings, Dr Emoto argued that the power of thoughts and words could change realities, which affect our health, both mental and physical. While this may seem far-fetched if true, what effect could this have on other people? It is perhaps worth thinking about this.

Don't Be Negative

The brain cannot ignore words it has to process the words first and then discount them later. If I said "Don't think of a pink elephant!" We first have to think about it and then delete it. This is worth remembering when talking, presenting and communicating with people. If you say to somebody:

> "Don't be nervous," or "I don't want you to feel uncomfortable"

Those words have to be brought to consciousness and then deleted. As words convey a message from one person to the other, the meaning associated with those words may cause people to become nervous or uncomfortable at an unconscious level. Let's explore this. We associate different feelings with different words. Try saying the word "relax" quietly and calmly a few times and notice how you feel. Now read this text slowly.

As you are reading this text, and reading the words and seeing the shapes of the letters, really focus on these words. And as you carry on reading these words and reading these sentences, the more you try not to think about it, the more you'll notice the increasing feeling of wanting to scratch.

Did you feel the urge to scratch? If so, carry on and do it now. This passage is based on work by Derren Brown, the British illusionist, in his book, "Tricks of the Mind". If you are like most people and felt the desire to scratch, then this shows the power of words and how we need to be careful with what we're saying and communicating when speaking.

COMMUNICATION BREAKDOWN

"The biggest problem in communication is the illusion that it is taking place."

This quote from George Bernard Shaw summarises things nicely. I'm sure many of us have had the experience of being on the phone to a call centre or helpline and becoming more and more exasperated as the person on the other end of the call seems unable to grasp what we're talking about. I've had many instances where we appear to be having a different conversation.

It illustrates how we attach our own meaning to communication. No matter how clear I attempt to be, a misunderstanding often occurs. I have found this frequently and it can be very frustrating. As communication is a two-way process, I have to accept part of the blame.

One way that I have found to make this more efficient is to summarise simply at the end of my request again what it is I'm looking for. On some occasions, I have asked the person to summarise what I'm looking for and then to repeat it back to me. They often still get it wrong and I have to explain it again. This I find improves things. Let's have a look now at how some of this miscommunication can occur.

The Lingo of Linguistics

We are now going to look at the world of linguistics and how language patterns work and how to use them to get what we want. Hypnotherapists and therapists are aware of language patterns and their power. It is beyond the scope of this book to deep dive into this. However, it is worth examining and it will assist us when speaking and communicating. Let's look at a very simple example.

Broken Windows

Consider the sentence:

"The window was broken."

Now on the surface, this seems a relatively straightforward sentence. However, if we look at this in more detail, it becomes apparent that this sentence is vague.

At an unconscious level, a "transderivational search" takes place. This means that we are attempting to attach meaning to a particular sentence. Let's think about this sentence again:

"The window was broken."

When was the window broken and by whom and using what? If we can't see the window, is it still broken? This requires brainpower similar to processing powering in a computer to analyse this. If we want to communicate a message effectively then we have to be as specific as possible.

If we want to allow people flexibility and more freedom of thought within a sentence, then we can become vaguer. You may have had the expression "artfully vague". If you want to become vaguer, use adjectives and adverbs. If you want to be specific, avoid them. Let's look at an example. If I said:

"I saw a car driving slowly down the street."

What does this mean? What car? Driven by whom? What does slowly mean? Is it 5 miles per hour (8kph), 10 miles per hour (16 kph) or 20 miles per hour (32 kph)? To understand the sentence, we have to attach a subjective meaning to it. This is advanced communication, but it is worth being aware that when using adjectives and adverbs they have no definitive meaning. Language can be so vague and confusing. This means that the meaning may not have been communicated as intended. Have you ever said something to somebody and then had to say afterwards:

"No, I didn't mean that, what I meant was..."

It had been interpreted differently to the intended meaning? Let's look at how confusion can occur with an example. Consider the sentence.

"I didn't say that you said that."

What does that mean? If we change the emphasis on each word in the sentence each time we say it, it gives the sentence a different meaning. Try it and notice this for yourself. Did you notice how the sentence sounded different and conveyed a different meaning depending on the emphasis?

Imagine that you are interviewing two candidates and the following two descriptions describe each candidate. Would you hire the person with the description at the top or the bottom? Read the two descriptions and go with your first impression.

Candidate 1

"She is intelligent, industrious, impulsive, critical, stubborn and envious."

Now let's look at the description of candidate two and see which candidate you prefer

Candidate 2

"She is envious, stubborn, critical, impulsive, industrious and intelligent."

Which candidate did you prefer? Candidate number one or candidate number two? Many people choose candidate number one. Did you? If not, that's ok.

If you didn't spot it, the descriptions contain the same words, but just in reverse order. Even though we know this, we are still more likely to attach more weight to the descriptions early in a sentence than those occurring later and choose candidate number one.

This is worth bearing in mind. Remember to put your most important points early in your description or message. The early words and numbers are priming expectations of what is coming.

Being Negative

Be careful when using negative language as it can become very confusing, for example:

"It wasn't what you didn't not do that wasn't the real issue, but rather it wasn't not doing what you shouldn't not have done that created the problem.

...welcome back after trying to understand that!

Don't "but"

Let's finish this chapter by sharing with you something very effective that I learned very on my career. That is to avoid using the word "but" where you can and to substitute with the word "and". The word *"but"* is a negation word and a divider and it discounts any previous statement that has been made. Let's look at an example.

*"I hear what you say, **but** I think we should..."*

This listener will interpret this as that you don't hear what they say. *Another example would be.*

*"It's a great idea **but...***

A much better way to do this is to use the word "and" because "and" links two ideas together. It is used in the world of hypnosis and in therapy to join concepts together. Read the two sentences below and notice how you feel.

*"It's a great idea, **but** we need more information to consider it properly."*

*"It's a great idea **and** we need more information to consider it properly."*

It's subtle, but it conveys a different message. Notice if you're using "but" and notice those that do and observe the effect it has on you and other people. Many people are, ***"yes but"*** people.

CHAPTER 14

Secrets to Asking Questions

Genuine Interest

Before looking at the different question types and how to use these, we need to make sure that our state is right. If you want to be seen as interesting, be interested. A useful state to be in is one of curiosity. It is also important to be congruent. There is no point in saying that sounds fascinating and using a flat tone of voice and showing no interest.

Let's Get Curious

If you can develop a natural curiosity with a mindset that you can learn from everybody, then this will help you. I heard a great phrase once which is that nobody knows enough to be a pessimist. Developing a genuine interest in other people and listening to what they have to say will help you build rapport with them. We can learn a lot from other people, as many have hobbies and interests and are experts in areas that you might never have come across before.

Expect Positive Outcome

Something that has worked well for me is to expect a positive outcome. This is not an arrogant attitude, but an air of expectancy. One thing is for sure, if you have negative air or beliefs it will do you no favours. Belief affects the outcome and the reader is referred to "Inside the Mind of Sales" where some quite unbelievable medical stories illustrate this.

Solid Foundations

Let's start with the basics. There are 5 main types of questions that we're going to look at:

1. Open Questions
2. Closed Questions
3. Rhetorical Questions
4. Command Questions
5. Tag Questions

Open Questions

Open questions elicit more information from somebody. These are questions that can't have a "yes" or "no" reply. Kipling said:

> "I keep six honest serving men (they taught me all I knew); their names are, What and Why and When and How and Where and Who."

These six words are powerful as they allow an exploration of someone's map to find out more information about them. It is still possible to get short answers, but not the "Yes" or "No" response. For example,

"What is the best way to use open questions?"

These are useful to use when you're wanting to get information from somebody and you want to open them up. This works well with people who are shy and more introverted.

Why Not?

One word of caution when using the "why" question. The "why" question can make people quite defensive because you are questioning their judgement and their criteria and value sets. It also causes them to justify their reasons for their actions. When using why we are challenging why they either bought a particular item or carried out a particular action.

To answer the question, revivification takes place as the person relives the experience. Then justification takes place as to why a particular item was bought or a specific action was carried out. If, for example, I was to ask you:

"Why did you buy that car?"

This can come across as criticising judgement? We may even get a response,

Why, what's wrong with it?

Notice how different this feels to

Where did you buy your car?

This implies that we like it and you would like to get one too. Rather than asking somebody why they bought a particular car, a much better and much softer way of asking is to say:

"What made you decide on that car? "

It's the same information you're asking for, just rephrased differently. If you want to put somebody under pressure, then you can use the question "why" but be aware that this triggers people to justify their behaviours and may come across as pushy and an interrogation.

Remember when we ask somebody a question about their action, their critical mind will rationalise their behaviour. For something to be perceived as true, the brain only has to perceive it as plausible. This is subtle, but as we have discussed when looking at stacking, we want to make sure we have as much layering as possible taking place.

Closed Questions

Closed questions are questions where the answer is either "yes" or "no". These questions are not good for eliciting information but are very useful in clarifying what somebody is saying. They are also useful if you want to narrow down the choices to either "yes or no". For example:

"Did you say that it was important to ask closed questions?"

If you have young children, they are the past masters of answering closed questions with a yes or no. It's good training for practising asking questions.

"Did you have fun at school today?"

"Yes"

"Did you learn anything new today?"

"No"

"Are you looking forward to going to the party?"

"Yes"

"Are you looking forward to Christmas?"

"Yes?"

If you want to get more information from them, you may have to say:

"What is it that you're looking forward to most about Christmas?"

This gives an extreme example of the effect of closed questions, but it is something to be aware of. Closed questions are very useful when you want to narrow down a person. They are also very useful when you're summarising and clarifying a particular point. I use closed questions a lot to check my understanding.

Closed questions are also very useful when you're dealing with someone who is very talkative and verbose and who goes off in many directions when speaking.

An example is:

"Just so that I can check my understanding, you are not happy with your current provider and it is under review. You are currently looking for a new provider and to narrow the selection process down to two alternatives. Is that correct?"

Closed questions are also useful when using the yes set. We will explore the yes set later. At some point, we want to get a yes or no. People who are aware of what you're doing will often not want to give a direct answer. Politicians are notorious for this.

Open questions are very useful when dealing with introverts and people who do not give a lot away.

Rhetorical Questions

Rhetorical questions are questions that do not require an answer and are used by professional communicators, public speakers, and politicians. We often use them in the middle of a talk or if somebody is starting a speech. Now, what is a rhetorical question you may be wondering? Well, I just gave you an example. They allow you to ask a question that you want to provide an answer to. For example:

"Now, why would we want to use rhetorical questions?"
"That is an excellent question, and I'm going to explain to you why we should use them."

This is a useful technique for a speaker or presenter or anyone communicating an idea or information to other people. The reason that this is so effective is that not only does it sound conversational, but it allows you to raise your own objections and answer them. In doing so, this creates the impression with the other person or the audience that you understand them. In communication and NLP, we call this a mind read. We are pacing what the other person or audience is thinking and yet we're allowing ourselves to answer the question.

It is also an excellent technique because allows you to get rid of any objections that you might anticipate by raising them yourself and then answering them yourself. They can also be used in everyday conversation too.

Rhetorical questions can open a talk or a speech and add more interest to a talk. Many people will open up a speech or a talk using a rhetorical question. If asked to deliver an impromptu speech (an impromptu speech is a speech or talk with very little notice) we can use these types of questions to gain us more time.

Many people panic and their mind goes blank when they are asked to talk without preparation. To give ourselves more time to think, simply repeat the question back to the person. You can add an acknowledgement in also. If someone asked you to talk about "Why should we use rhetorical questions" you could say:

"That's a great question, (acknowledgement) now why should we use rhetorical questions?" (repetition).

We could also use:

"That's an interesting question," or "What a great question."

This gives your unconscious mind time to provide us with all the information that you need. Anyone can learn this, it is just a matter of practise.

A variation on rhetorical questions is asking a rhetorical question based on a statement that you may have made that may be confusing or need clarity. This is an excellent method to use when in conversation or when delivering a presentation involving technical details. Let's look at an example. If I said:

"It's important to introduce a pattern interrupt when you are delivering a speech or a presentation"

We then simply add,

"Now you may wonder what a pattern interrupt is. Well, let's explore this."

Once you get into the habit of this, you will do it unconsciously, without even having to think about it.

Command Questions

Command questions are statements that sound like questions. They can be used very effectively to make the questioning sound more conversational. They are commands that are tagged on the front of questions.

Command questions are questions that often begin with:

"Tell me", "Show me", "Explain to me" and "Let me understand."

These are often immediately followed by an open question. For example:

"Tell me, what is it that excites you most that you do in your spare time?

A word of caution when using command questions. When speaking, the emphasis is on the open question word, "what", and not on the words, "tell me". In the above example, the words, *"Tell me"* would be said fairly quickly, a short pause taken, and then the emphasis is placed on the second part of the sentence:

"Tell me, <u>what</u> is it that excites you most about the business that you are in?"

Tag Questions

The next type of question that we are going to consider are tag questions. Tag questions are questions that are tagged on to the end of a statement to get a yes or no response. Tag questions include the phrases such as:

"Isn't it, doesn't it, can't you, mustn't we, shouldn't we, won't it, and don't you?"

Tag questions are useful because they can get people to say "yes" or "no"
For example:

Even though you know that I am using a tag question, it's very difficult to resist, isn't it?

I've just used the tag question here. Presenters and professional speakers use tag questions. The main reason is that it gets the people involved and is more conversational. The response to a tag question is either "yes" or "no".

If you are using tag questions to elicit a "yes" response, the more times that a person says yes, then the more likely they are to agree with you. This is called *"the yes set"* and anything that makes life easier for us has to be a good thing, doesn't it?.........yes!!

Tag questions are also very useful because people may not say yes, but when talking to an individual, group or when online, if you are sharp of eye, you will notice a nodding of the head. This occurs unconsciously if they agree with you. When speaking to a group or online, this is helpful. This helps to find out who are the friends and the foes are and who agrees with your content and who doesn't. Which is useful *isn't it?*

The key when using tag questions is not to overuse them. We want to make our communication natural and for this to happen below the level of awareness. If you are overusing tag questions, somebody will pick up on this and it becomes annoying. Let's look at an example of how to use tag questions. Let's take the statement first:

"If you look at this chart, it shows just how strong the performance has been."

This is quite a disassociated statement, as the other person does not have to engage much. Making a simple change gets the "yes set" started:

"If you look at this chart, you can see just how strong the performance has been, <u>can't you?</u>"

"Performance is important, <u>isn't it?</u> Have a look at how our investment has performed. It looks very strong, <u>doesn't it?</u>"

Use this sparingly and always remember to have a desire to connect with someone and to do the best for them. We don't want to come across as a manipulator. After all, we all want a win-win situation, *don't we?*

Resistance

People resist what they are told and accept what they conclude. If you tell somebody to do something, there is a little voice inside them called the "F You factor". We covered this earlier. If I was to say:

"Can you make me a coffee, please?"

There is a little voice that says: "F you!"

"Make your own coffee. Who are you to tell me to make you a coffee?"

Now, if we can put a reason around why someone should make a coffee, it becomes more plausible and people are more likely to comply. So if I said:

"Can you get me a coffee please because I'm just about to jump on a webinar with a very important client?"

You would probably think that sounds reasonable and would do it. The reason only has to be plausible for the brain to believe it. This is worth remembering when asking questions. Always contextualise and give a reason for asking the question. We will explore this in more detail next.

Give Me a Reason Why

This principle of giving people a "reason why" is powerful and increases compliance with your request. One way that we can do this when asking questions is to explain in simple terms why we are asking the question. If I met you for the first time and asked:

"What's your major criteria for selecting a particular product?"

Part of you may think:

"Well, actually, it's none of your business."

However, if you can contextualise this and say:

"In order that I may understand your business better,"

and possibly add:

"So that I'm not wasting any of your time, what are the major criteria you use for selecting.....?"

And then ask the question. If somebody was to stop you in the street and ask you if you would mind answering a few questions in a survey. How would you react? Well, first, they haven't addressed what's in it for you and second, they haven't given you any reason why you should do it. In these circumstances, most people would say no. If, however, they were to contextualise it and give a reason why they should do it, then you are more likely to comply.

Imagine that you were walking down a street and there was a lot of litter or trash. If I were to stop you and ask you if you have a couple of minutes to answer some questions many people would say no. However if I explain I am organising a campaign to help make the streets cleaner and more pleasant for everybody and then ask you to complete the survey to help with this then you are more likely to assist.

SOFTENING THINGS

Language Softeners

Language softeners are phrases that can make questions seem more conversational and less intrusive. When finding out the information, we don't want to make it seem like an interrogation. Think about language softeners as wrapping paper. They dress the question up to make it seem more appealing. We can use this principle of giving a reason with language softeners. If I wanted to find out what somebody's biggest challenge is in their business, I could simply ask:

> *"What is the biggest challenge that you face in your business?"*

There is nothing wrong with asking this question. The only issue is that it is quite direct and has little context. Ask too many of these types of questions and it becomes like an interrogation.

Let's look at how we can soften this. We all like context. Have you ever had a conversation with somebody and they spoke randomly and you got confused? They may have assumed that you know the context that they are speaking about? It's quite annoying as we desperately try to make sense and put some context and meaning around what they are saying.

A better way to ask questions is to use a language softener in front. This does two things:

1. It adds context
2. It provides a reason for answering

An example of this would be:

"So that I can understand your business better, what is the biggest challenge that you face in your business at the moment with product distribution?"

Just Presupposing

A way to soften this further is through the use of presuppositions. For the listener to make sense of the sentence, then part of the statement is presupposed and presumed to be true. It is easier to illustrate this with an example:

"When you buy this product, you may decide to upgrade"

In this sentence, it is presupposed that a purchase is going to take place. The question is whether an upgrade is going to take place.

Let's go back to our original example and this time we are going to add the phrase "Would you be able to let me know?".

"So that I can understand your business better, would you be able to let me know what is the biggest challenge that you face with sales distribution?"

In this statement, it is presupposed that the person will answer the question. The focus is on whether or not they will *be able to let you know*. People in sales will use this. For example, if I was to say to you:

"I wonder whether we should look at the solution now or later."

It is presumed that we are going to look at the solution the question is whether we are looking at it now or later. This technique works equally well in social situations.

Clarify

If you are speaking in front of an audience or to a group of people, a great technique that we can use when somebody asks a question is to repeat the question back. Many people, when they're attending a presentation, talk or speech may have drifted off and lost concentration. If someone else has just asked a question and we have not heard it, this is annoying and we want to know what was said. It causes mild confusion. The brain does not like confusion. Repeating the question allows everyone to get involved.

Summarise

Many people when they ask a question will include several long statements and sometimes it's quite difficult to know exactly what they're asking, particularly if they are verbose or wordy. The way around this is to listen to what they're saying and then to summarise and repeat back to them while giving them a reason. For example:

"Just so that a can I check my understanding, you are asking about......?"

In this case, we are using closed questions to make sure that we narrow them down to the point or information that they want to know more about.

CHAPTER 15

Avoiding the Mistakes

H aving discussed the different types of questions and questioning techniques in the previous chapter, let us look at areas where people make mistakes and how we can fix them. This applies to business, management, sales your personal and intimate lives. In fact, in any situation.

THE BIGGEST QUESTION MISTAKES

Questions when used incorrectly can impact negatively on both you and your message. There are different categories of common mistakes that people make when asking and when using questions. Let's look at those now in detail.

The Spanish Inquisition

When people first learn about asking questions and particularly open questions, many take this too literally and start interrogating people. They are unaware of the effect of asking too many why questions. Think about this, imagine I started asking you questions. *"What is your name?"* and then you answer. I then ask: *"Where are you from?"* and you answer and then: *"What do you do for a living?"* and you answer. Around about this point you may feel as if I'm just asking too many questions.

There are things we can do to avoid this. When we ask somebody a question and they answer the question simply, just comment about the answer. We will cover this later in part two of the book and how to best do this.

Question and Answerers

Question and answers are people who ask a question and then answer it themselves. Sometimes, this occurs when people are nervous. Let's give an example of this:

> *"What sort of things do you look for in a supplier? Is it price customer service, product support, that sort of thing?"*

> *"What is it you like most about working here? Is it the atmosphere, the people, the culture, the opportunities?"*

Now that I've pointed this out, you may think people wouldn't possibly do this, but next time you're listening to people asking questions, just notice how many people do this.

The Statement Makers

The "statement makers" fall into two categories:

1. The first type is people who make a statement without asking a question. An example is:

> *"Communication skills are very important at work and we all need to learn these for different occasions and working with different people."*

2. The second type is people who are statement makers. They make a wordy statement, then follow this with a question. They aim to demonstrate how clever they are by showing knowledge, understanding and to show off to everybody else in the group before asking the question.

Answerer and Questioners

"Answerers and Questioners" answer the question first and then turn it into a question. An example would be:

"Presumably you like watching thrillers as part of a box set featuring well know actors. Would that be correct?"

Journalists are guilty of this. You can also use this as a trap for people. If you make a statement and then ask a question and the person does not rebut the statement, then the statement has been accepted. An example of trapping somebody would be:

"Crime in this city is escalating out of control. What are you doing about it?"

Question, Yes & I

"Question, Yes & I", these people ask a question and immediately, on hearing the answer, start talking about themselves. Let's look at an example.

Questioner

"Have you ever been to Sicily?"

Answerer

"Yes."

Questioner

"I've been to Sicily too, and I had a fabulous time. It was a friend of mine that recommended going there. He recommended a magnificent hotel to stay at and said that I would love it......etc.

People are unlikely to be interested in any of this information.

The Apologetic Questioner

Apologetic questioners lack confidence and apologise for asking a question. There is a difference between being polite and showing no authority or command of the conversation.
An example is:

"If it's not too much trouble, I don't want to appear as if I'm asking anything out of turn and if you don't feel comfortable telling me this information, that's ok. Would it be possible, if you don't mind, to let me know a little about your business if it's not too inconvenient?"

The Interrupters

These are people who ask a question and before the answer is complete, interrupt and ask another question. Sometimes they may even interrupt to talk about themselves again.

If someone has asked you a question and doesn't let you answer, but interrupts, it is very annoying. Somebody may put up with one or two interruptions, but if this is ongoing, it will annoy them. There are three exceptions where an interruption is acceptable:

1. If they used a term or an abbreviation which is one that we're not familiar with, or we're confused by. If, for example, they use the acronym BDF and we don't know what the BDF stands for, simply saying "BDF" with a

rising tone allows for clarification without appearing intrusive.

2. If someone keeps talking and goes on and on without a gap in speaking.
3. If the person keeps going off on a tangent and we want to bring them back to the point.

Be very careful when interrupting people as they don't like it. The best approach is to allow someone to finish and to minimise your interruptions.

Be Careful With Why

Be very careful when using the question "why". Try to avoid using it altogether and we have covered this earlier. There is an exception to using the question "why?" and this is where you want somebody to justify their behaviour. Here "why" is a useful question to ask. However, just remember that whenever you ask "why" you are exposing somebody's criteria and values, which are laid down often unconsciously.

PART TWO

Getting It Together

CHAPTER 16

Getting Set Up

We covered a lot of the theory about communication and talking to people, together with the science associated with it, in the first part of this book. I would recommend re-reading it again to ensure that you have a thorough understanding before putting the theory into practice. It is just a matter of practise and anyone can do it.

Communication with somebody begins way before you even speak to them. The state you are in, the expected outcome, and your desire to communicate with that person will all affect the outcome.

Learning from Sherlock Holmes

Before talking to somebody, there are many clues about that individual that will help to improve the interaction. If you have observed the person walking, what type of walk do they have? Do they lead with their head or with the chest?

Many people who are academics or more cerebral lead with their head first. We may think of the old-fashioned university professor walking with his body tilted forward and his head looking down. People who lead with their chest first are more heart centric. Once we have spotted this body language pattern, it gives us a clue how we should conduct the conversation. Should we be making our conversation more logical and factual, or should we be making it more emotional? Is their walk quick or slow? Is it high energy with a spring in the step or more subdued? Remember the principle, that the outer expression reflects the inner thought.

Give Me Some Space

How much space does the person take up? We discussed that extrovert and confident people take up more space and that introverted and less confident people make themselves smaller. If you are meeting people in a large social gathering, introverted people are often at the side of the room and extroverted people are in the centre. The language gives us a clue with the expression "being the centre of attention".

Watching the Body

Body language is a big topic and the reader is recommended to refer to the work by the author in the book "Body Language How to Read Any Body" for an in-depth understanding of all the nuances involved in nonverbal communication. Let's look at the main things that we can look at to give us more clues.

What does the person's posture look like? Is it upright and how big is the space between their feet when they're standing? Many people, when they want to make themselves appear more confident, will widen the space between their feet. Think of the typical policeman stance.

What Are You Looking At?

We can also look at a person's eye contact. Confident and dominant people control their body language and they reflect this with their controlled head and eye movement. This also includes the blink rate.

I have observed that many intellectual people, when they're trying to communicate an idea or when involved in a debate, will often increase their blink rate unconsciously. We associate this with introverted intellectuals and can show that deep thinking is taking place.

When looking at their eyes, do they hold your gaze or do their eyes fleet away? Confident people are very comfortable making eye contact and find this a natural thing to do.

Looking At the Toys

If we meet people in their own home, many clues show their hobbies, interests and what is important to them in terms of values.

If we're meeting somebody in a business environment and we see lots of photos of the family, then we know that this is high on their criteria and values. Perhaps we may see them wearing an expensive watch. Is their clothing conservative or more flamboyant?

It is worth sharpening our awareness skills to see if there are any indications of their hobbies or interests. For example, if somebody has a picture of themselves in the background on a golf course, it is a pretty safe bet that golf ranks high on their priority list. If somebody is wearing a necktie, it may have the logo of a club that they belong to.

It is worth getting into the habit when we are out and about in everyday life of sharpening our awareness skills and trying to gain as much information as we can from somebody without asking them questions. Of course, we will not always get it right. However, the idea is to get as many clues as possible and develop a deep curiosity.

STATE TRAINING

Training Awareness

In part one of the book, we covered the principle of entrainment, which is how people get in synch with each other. We also looked at how people form reality both internal and external together with the importance of the heart and communication and developing an intense desire to get to know someone using the "R+ method". Let's do an exercise now to practise training awareness and moving it.

Place your right hand out in front of you and place your awareness inside the tip of your forefinger. Imagine that you are actually inside of your forefinger. Now imagine that you are breathing in and out through the tip of your forefinger. For some people, this may take a bit of practise and for others, they will find it quite easy to do. Now notice the temperature around your forefinger. As you keep your attention on the tip of your finger, you may notice a pulse. Once you have done this for a few minutes, stop the exercise and we will move on to training the heart.

Training the Heart

Heartmath Institute has established heart coherence between two people and this can occur in animals, too. When we are training the heart, we're wanting to leave our logical brains out of the way to focus on emotion and feelings. Some of you may think, well, I'm not an emotional person, but everybody has been excited before. Even the act of not being emotional is an act of emotion. Let's do an exercise to become more heart centric.

Take a few moments to relax and take a few deep breaths and breathe out any tension. Now place your attention on your heart. To focus your attention on your heart and imagine that you are breathing in and out through your heart. Now recall a time in your life when you were at your most charismatic and confident. If you can't recall a memory, then simply make something up. We know that the brain processes information in the same way irrespective of whether it is experienced or vividly imagined.

Now imagine that there is a hatch door in front of your heart. Allow this hatch door to open and imagine filling up the room with a colour that represents that memory of that communication. Go with your first impression and if you don't have a memorable one, then just pretend. Be playful. This is the secret to success. Keep imagining the colour emanating from your heart and hold this image for a couple of minutes. Before I am doing a presentation or a talk, I use this technique. I use the colour purple, but you could choose whichever colour is best for you. This is called the "Heart Trigger".

Now of course we're not emitting a colour it is all imaginary. However, as we explored earlier, the unconscious mind is the one moving the bus. It responds to imagery, emotion and repetition and this is an excellent way to help get you in the correct state.

Play Pretend

Another way to get into the right state is to imagine that the person you are meeting is someone else. If you want to come across as more friendly, imagine meeting an old friend. If you want to come across as more business-like, imagine you are meeting with your favourite boss.

CONTROLLING YOUR BODY LANGUAGE

We have looked at being aware of the body language of the person to who we are speaking, but we must also learn to control our body language. Using the heart trigger method described above and using imagining meeting an old friend technique will help us get in the right state.

We can also use our body position to affect our state. If we want to feel confident, then we adopt confident body language. I'm sure many of us have seen what I call the master criminal pose. We see this James Bond film where we see the bond villain standing looking at a map of the world with his hands behind his back and his feet wider apart.

You can adopt a power pose similar to this or something that works for you. Just think of a time when you are at your most confident, you're most invincible, and adopt that body position and hold it for a few minutes. Then notice how you feel. This works by using the mind-body connection which we have explored.

Avoid displaying signs of nervous body language by shuffling or putting your fingers or hands near your face. For more details of the meanings of various face blocking behaviours, please refer to the author's book Body Language How to Read Any Body where this is explored in great detail.

TIME TO APPROACH

Don't Stand So Close To Me

When you see somebody, it is better to approach them from the side or at an angle. This is less threatening than approaching from the front or square on. Approaching square on can come across as being combative. The language gives us a clue as we talk about "squaring up" to an opponent and about "facing our adversary" or being "on opposite sides" of an argument. If people don't agree, they will often sit opposite each other.

When approaching somebody, don't get too close. Each of us has our space and there are different zones. There is the business zone, personal zone and intimate zones. These are shown in Fig 4. (Chapter 12).

I once worked with somebody who had a habit of getting far too close to people. When watching various interactions, you could see people moving back to gain more space. As they did so, this person would move even closer. Accompanying this encroachment of personal space were frequent uninvited touches and elbowing. It was very uncomfortable to watch. This person had very low awareness skills and did not know the message that was being communicated.

To the Left or the Right

We want to stack as many things in our favour as we can. One way that we can add to the stack is how we position ourselves. If a person is right-handed, then they will like you better if you stand on the right-hand side. The same applies to seating. One way to work out if somebody is right or left-handed is to notice which hand they hold a cup when they're drinking. Other clues might be a watch on their right wrist.

As most people are right-handed, it is better to stand on the right. If you suddenly find that they are left-handed, you can make an excuse and move to the other side of the person by perhaps by saying that there is a reflection catching your eye.

I CAN SEE YOU

The eyes have been described as the windows to the soul. The eyes can reveal a lot of information about what a person is thinking. They are very useful to observe. The eyes can convey a lot of information through eye movement and when accompanied by other body movements.

When two people meet and make eye contact, they find themselves in an unusual situation. They want to look at each other and yet they also want to look away. This can cause a series of sometimes complex eye movements. When we meet somebody for the first time, we are sizing each other up. We are trying to find out if someone is a friend or foe. We also want to find out if what they are saying is of interest and beneficial to us and whether we find them attractive. If you observe carefully, you will see this process taking place.

The rules of this glancing behaviour are complicated. If we hold their gaze too long, this can create the wrong impression. If we don't hold it long enough, then equally this can have an adverse effect.

Hypnotists are aware of the power of holding eye contact for a long time. Many have perfected the art of the hypnotic gaze to hypnotise people. Many of us will have had the experience of somebody who holds a gaze just a little too long. We will also have experienced the opposite of someone who doesn't hold the gaze long enough and whose eyes are darting about all over the place. A method that works well to avoid the hypnotic gaze is to stare at a spot just below the two eyebrows. If we are attracted to someone, we have this conflict of wanting to look at someone that we find attractive. However, we also have the feeling that we don't want to make this obvious.

Eye Power

Let's have a look at eye contact when dealing with status. You may have come across the expression "eyeballing". We see this when boxers are staring at each other at close range before a fight. Holding a gaze is a sign of dominance and the one that looks away gives away power. Let's look at an example of the gaze in everyday behaviour. Think about a situation when a boss is displeased with an employee's behaviour or performance. The boss holds eye contact with the employee and confronts them. The employee then justifies themselves. The boss continues to glare at the employee. In a sign of submission, the employee cannot hold the gaze and will look down or away. The employee is literally "losing face". The converse is when we hear people saying that we want to allow them "to save face".

Expressions often reflect the physical aspects of behaviour. In the example above, the boss may say, "I'm going to be keeping a close eye on you". Or he may say I am going to be "watching you very closely going forward!" The language is telling us what he is going to be doing.

Sideways glances

Holding a gaze a fraction too long can indicate finding another person appealing or attractive. If we are in a social gathering, we may find somebody appealing. We don't want to display lecherous facial expressions and behaviours, but we may want to hold someone's gaze a little longer.

The converse is also true. If there is somebody that we dislike, we try to hide any facial and body expressions that could show this. As a result, we will look at the person less and less. Phrases are often very true. You may have heard somebody say, "I just couldn't bear to even look at him". This translates into looking at him causes me discomfort. Most people want to move away from discomfort towards pleasure. You may notice that if someone does not like you, or like what you are saying, they will look at you less. This becomes more obvious as emotions increase.

Under these more moderate conditions, emotions can be controlled and the outward display of emotion is reduced. We may see false smiles. You may have heard people saying that "she is just so false". This is an unconscious response. People often find it difficult to analyse exactly why somebody is false. They just say there is something about them. We may even see nodding, accompanying the smile as people attempt to appear congruent. Smiles are easier to fake. We have more control and awareness over them than we do our glances. We may not be aware of the change in our glances. However, gradually the amount of time we spend looking at a person who we don't like gradually decreases. The brevity of the gaze gives the game away.

Getting the Eye

Rather than looking at the smiling and nodding, watch the eyes for clues. Eye glancing movements are important and looking at the whites of the eyes makes this more obvious. We have the expression "staring into the whites of the eyes". We can sharpen our awareness by noticing people who engage in conversation and dancing of the eyes. People will initially look at you. They will often look away and most times, they are accessing different parts of their internal reality, as discussed earlier. This carries on until they hand the conversation back to the original person. This is by a returning gaze. It is the length of time that this returning gaze lasts that gives clues.

To look for more clues with gaze behaviour, think about the expression, "He looked shifty". This often conveys someone who cannot hold your gaze and has shifty eyes. This comes back to the basic principle of inner thoughts being conveyed in the external expression.

Where Should I Look?

There are some protocols that we can adopt when knowing where to look. Let's have a look at three different gaze zones as shown in Fig. 5. There is the business gaze, the social gaze and the intimate gaze. Many of us will have had the experience where someone has gazed in the wrong area. When they do, it can make us feel uncomfortable. If you want to have some fun, next time you speak to a friend or someone you know well, just stare at a spot a few inches above their head. They will turn around and look behind them and ask what are you looking at? Let's look at the three zones. While nothing is cast in stone, it is advisable to be careful with the gazes. Many men often use intimate gaze far too quickly with unintended consequences.

The Three Gazes

Business Gaze

Social Gaze

Intimate Gaze

Fig.5

SMILE AS IF YOU MEAN IT

Smiling is an incredibly powerful gesture. The language gives us a clue, "smile and the world smiles with you". People have learned the importance of a smile and the need to display it. This has meant that many people have learned a fake smile. Have you ever met somebody and while they were smiling, it felt as if they weren't pleased to meet you and it was a fake smile? Our smile must be genuine. Let's look at the difference between a real smile and a fake smile.

Researchers have discovered that humans have a fake and real smile. A real smile or "Duchenne smile" appears primarily because of the action of two muscles. When these two muscles work together, the corners of the mouth are drawn up and a crinkling around the outer edges of the eyes occurs, causing crow's feet. These muscles are the *zygomaticus major*, which stretches from the corner of the mouth to the cheekbone, and the *orbicularis oculi*, which surrounds the eye. It is important to make sure that our smile is genuine and to avoid a false smile and to practice if necessary.

A fake smile can be referred to as a mouth only smile. With a real smile, we see crinkling of the eyes, lifting and symmetry. This means crinkling of the skin to the side of the eyes, a lifting of the sides of the mouth and an asymmetrical smile.

Women smile more than men. For men when interacting with women, they should smile more, and for women when in a corporate environment dominated by men, reduce your smiling. If you are female and you choose to smile, research has shown that women who are slower to smile in a corporate environment are perceived as more credible.

Pleased To See You

I remember when I was at school there was one particularly popular person who had lots of friends and that everybody seemed to like. It intrigued me how he did this. Then, after observing him in many situations, I spotted he was always pleased to see somebody. This came across as genuine and the effect on people was hypnotic.

CHAPTER 17

Starting a Conversation

Some people feel very uncomfortable at the thought of meeting someone they don't know. If this is in an unknown environment, this can add to the discomfort. In this section, we're going to explore and give a framework for how to meet people and start a conversation. We will look at an approach that you can use that works every time and in any situation. Everybody is different and some people break the rules. However, it is worth knowing the rules before deciding to break them.

Conversations with Strangers

We've looked at searching for clues, analysing body language patterns and how to approach people. Let's now look at starting a conversation.

What Shall We Talk About?

This is easy. What is everybody's favourite topic of conversation? Look in the mirror for the answer. That's right, it's us. The secret to making people like you is by showing how much you like them!

STAGE 1

If we were to go up to a stranger and start asking questions with no small talk or any preamble, many would find this unusual and would be less likely to engage in conversation. There is a process that we go through as we get to know people and build trust with them. The more trust and more rapport we build then the more dialogue that you will have. What do we do with people that we don't like? That's right, we ignore them. Three questions to avoid are:

"Where are you from?"

"What do you do?"

"Do you come here often?"

We can ask these questions interspersed in a conversation discretely later on, but this is not the best way to start a conversation.

The easiest way to start a conversation is using one of three topics. When using this, it pays to sharpen your awareness skills.

1. Location
2. Occasion
3. Personal (with caution)

LOCATION

To begin with, we don't want to ask questions directly about them but to make a comment about our surroundings. For example, suppose that we were meeting somebody in a hotel venue or at the conference centre. We would pay attention to what we observe and comment on what we are experiencing.

I was recently in a large office block in the centre of London, which housed several businesses. When I first entered the building, there was a beautiful aroma. This is quite unusual and the only time that I had experienced this before was when I was in Geneva in Switzerland. To engage in small talk with the receptionist, I immediately commented on how wonderful the smell was and the impact it has on visitors. Having made the observation, I could then ask a question. "Where is that beautiful smell coming from?" The receptionist appreciated the fact that I had noticed this and immediately told me about a special machine and went off to find a card with the name of the company on it.

We may want to comment on something visual. It is worth paying particular attention when you are on a video call or if in somebody's office and you see a picture on the wall. There may be a particular reason for that choice of picture. The location may represent a special memory, or they may have painted it themselves. It may just be a random picture, but it is a conversation opener.

Let's look at how we can comment on sounds that we may hear. If we find ourselves in a venue to attend a training session and we hear sounds coming from another room, we could comment:

"That sounds like they're having fun in there. I hope that our training program is going to be as much fun."

We could also add in some humour, for example:

"That sounds like they're having a lot of fun in there. I wonder if the comedian was expensive."

This type of humour is ice-breaking humour. People are unlikely to be rolling around the ground with laughter, but it is often enough to draw a wry smile if delivered the correct way. The key is to comment on the environment that you both can experience and agree on. We don't want to make a statement that they could disagree with, for example:

> "I wish they would turn that music off I can't stand classical music."

Because the other person may say:

> "Well, actually I quite like it."

We have immediately formed a barrier. It is impossible to cover every scenario, but if you use the principles with practice, it will become easy.

How to Practice

We have focused so much in this book on the need to sharpen our awareness and to shift away from internal thoughts and our internal voice and focus on the external environment. One of the best ways to practise using location statements is to do this in our everyday life. We can do this in the different locations that we encounter. Let's use a couple of examples to illustrate this.

Imagine that we find ourselves in a coffee shop or a cafe. This is a suitable environment to practise in, as many of our senses can be stimulated. We would expect to experience the smell of coffee, the sound of a coffee machine, the process of somebody making the coffee, cakes on display and many other things. We can incorporate these observations into our initial statement. It is easy. We just have to adopt a state of curiosity. The examples beneath will make this clearer:

"Those cakes look delicious and very tempting." (opener)

"Which one is the most popular?" (open question)

"Which one would you recommend?" (asking advice)

OCCASION

The "occasion technique" if used properly, is a version of,

"Why are you here?" or "What are you doing here?"

However, if we ask those questions directly without a language softener, we risk someone thinking,

"Well, actually, it's none of your business!"

In this situation, we need to use a language softener and some pacing, which we described in Chapter 14. Let's have a look at how we could do this.

Language Softener

Instead of asking: "Why are you here?" We could add some language softeners around this to make it sound less intrusive.

"I hope that you don't mind me asking, (language softener) I was wondering (curiosity) what was it that brought you here today?"

If it is in a social situation or perhaps we may want to talk to somebody that we find attractive who is with a group of friends. Instead of asking a predictable question such as:

"Why are you here?" or "Do you come here often?"

We can add some pacing (describe something verifiable), give a reason for your question and then describe what is going on together with some language softeners.

"You two seem like you're having a great time (pace). I hope you don't mind me asking (softener), I'm curious, (giving a reason & curiosity), what do you like most about this bar?" (presupposition that they like the bar).

STAGE 2 ECHO & COMMENT

Echo

When we looked at rapport, we discovered that the most important words that a person hears are the ones that they have just said. We also discovered that saying back the very words that they have just said will ensure that we are in the right representational system (sight, sound, feeling, taste and smell). For example, if they said:

"I have come into town to have a <u>look</u> around"

We would repeat back:

"So you have come into town to have a <u>look</u> around?"

When you use the echo technique, expect to hear the word "yes" together with some head nodding. There is nothing wrong with repeating back the sentence in its entirety, but many of us struggle to remember it and its far better to pick out a few points in a longer sentence and echo this back to the person. Getting into the habit of this will improve your listening skills.

Comment

The next stage after someone answers your initial question and echoing, is to comment on the answer they have given to your question. This is a brief comment. It is not an opportunity to talk about yourself.

Let's look at an example of the right way to do this and an example of the wrong way to do this. Let's return to our two example questions again. As a reminder, here they are.

Question

"I hope you don't mind me asking. I am curious and was wondering what brought you here today?"

Answer

"I work in financial regulation and I wanted to attend this presentation to get an update on the regulations."

Echo

"So you work in financial regulation and you wanted to attend this presentation to get an update on the regulations?"

Comment

"I can imagine this is a complicated field (pace) and is ever-evolving (pace) and must be difficult to keep up." (pace)

Next Question

Then ask another question. Let's look at a second example.

Question

"You two seem like you're having a great time (pace). I hope you don't mind me asking. I'm curious, (giving a reason) is there a big celebration going on? What brought you here tonight?"

Answer

"I am here with my friend for a few drinks. We haven't seen each other for a while and she has just received a promotion and we're out to celebrate."

We can either repeat the entire sentence back to them or we can shorten it if you feel more comfortable with this. In the second example, the reply is much longer. We may want to shorten the echo slightly. For example, we may say:

Echo

"So you are out with your friend for a few drinks to celebrate your her promotion?"

Comment

"Congratulations, you must be delighted (pace). There is nothing quite like catching up with friends over a few drinks (pace). It is one of life's great pleasures, isn't it?" (Pace, tag question).

In the last sentence, we have added a couple of powerful language patterns. We have mentioned great pleasures. The word pleasure primes people unconsciously. We have also added the tag question at the end of the sentence, which causes people to say "yes" and automatically start nodding their heads. This is a powerful rapport building technique. Nodding the head and saying yes is associated with positivity and sets up the yes set (Chapter 14).

The Next Question

This is the part where most people trip up. They don't know what to ask next. With practise this will become easier and easier. The brain works with associations. When I'm coaching people, we use a technique that I call "riffing." We use this technique to help people with their impromptu speaking. I pick out random topics for somebody to speak on, and then we swap and they give me a random topic and we play this a bit like the game of tennis. Once you know that the brain learns by association and that you can trust your unconscious mind to provide you with all the words that you need, it becomes very easy. We need to practise this just as all excellent communicators do. They have spent a lot of time observing and refining what they do.

So what is the best way to ask the second question in the "question, echo, comment, question format"? (rhetorical question) We want to keep the conversation general and not ask personal questions just yet. It's a good idea to link your next question to what they originally said. Let's go back to our two examples again and remind ourselves of the answers. We have echoed, commented and now we are moving on to question two.

EXAMPLE 1

Question 1

"I hope you don't mind me asking. I am curious and was wondering what brought you here today?"

Answer

"I work in financial regulation and I wanted to attend this presentation to get an update on the regulations."

Echo

"So you work in financial regulation and you wanted to attend this presentation to get an update on the regulations?"

Comment

"I can imagine this is a complicated field (pace) and is ever-evolving (pace) and must be difficult to keep up." (pace)

Question 2

"What are the biggest issues that you face in financial regulation and what are you hoping to get out of today?"

We have used open questions to open the person up.

EXAMPLE 2

Question 1

"You two seem like you're having a great time (pace). I hope you don't mind me asking. I'm curious, (giving a reason) is there a big celebration on what brought you here tonight?"

Answer

"I am here with my friend for a few drinks. We haven't seen each other for a while and she has just received a promotion and we're out to celebrate."

We can either repeat the entire sentence back to them or we can shorten it if you feel more comfortable with this. In the second example, the reply is much longer. Here, we may want to shorten the echo slightly. For example, we may say:

Echo

"So you are out with your friend for a few drinks to celebrate your her promotion?"

Comment

"Congratulations, you must be delighted. (Pace) There is nothing quite like catching up with friends over a few drinks. (pace) It is one of life's great pleasures isn't it?" (Pace, tag question)

Question 2

"I'm curious, what made you choose this bar?"

If you want to try and work out if someone is local, you only have to ask:

"Have you had to travel far?"

While this is a closed question, and you know the answer is going to be yes or no, people will usually expand on this. The benefit of using this type of question is that we learn whether they are local and we can use this to comment. If they are not local, we can say:

"It's always great to go to new places, variety is the spice of life isn't it?"

If they are local, we can say,

"It's great being able to nip out for a quick drink without having to travel far, isn't it?"

Using the tag questions at the end starts the yes set. This is a good question to ask rather than saying, where are you from. It is more subtle, and it allows people to introduce as much or as little information as they want to. Invariably, they will tell you where they're from and that gives you a lead into the next question and the conversation can develop.

GETTING PERSONAL

We need to be careful if we're making a comment that is not too personal to the person. I prefer to make an observational comment about the location first and, if this is not possible, then the occasion.

This is only guidance, and it will vary from person to person. Making a personal comment works well is if somebody is wearing something slightly unusual and they know it. They have chosen to wear something unusual to be noticed and to stand out. By acknowledging this, people often appreciate it. Somebody may have a nice watch or a necklace that you admire, or perhaps they have a handkerchief in their top pocket that is of a particular Scottish tartan. Commenting on these together with an exploratory question can work well.

I would urge caution when making comments about clothing, particularly with women in a business environment. However, if you comment on an unusual necklace and frame the reason for the comment, then this can be accepted. Let's have a look now at some ways that we can make personal comments without coming across as too intimate. By mentioning that something is unique and using the phrase, *"I really like...."* This shows somebody that you recognise their particular choice of accessory. Let's look at an example now:

"I really like that necklace that you're wearing it's unique. I've not seen anything like that before. Do you mind me asking, what stone is that in the middle?"

"I really like that pocket handkerchief. What tartan is that I've not seen that before?"

We would then follow the process as before with question, echo, comment, and question.

CHAPTER 18

The Introduction

At some point when we are speaking to somebody, we have to introduce ourselves. If this is an informal conversation, I prefer to do this after we've spoken for a little while. In a social situation, I usually say:

"I should have introduced myself. I'm Derek, great to meet with you. What's your name?"

I extend my arm out, and a handshake takes place. This comes after a small period of small talk when you're speaking to somebody.

If this is a business environment, it is worth introducing yourself early on, together with your position and what you do within a firm. This may even include your location if you're working for an international firm. The reason to do this is that we can recall from the earlier chapters that the confused mind always says no and people are in a state of confusion if they don't have context. Once people know who you are, what you do and where you're from, it validates the reason to speak to you.

The Handshake

The correct handshake is to have your hand at right angles to the floor. Extend your hand out in front of you with your knuckles on the right-hand side and your palm on the left-hand side. When shaking hands, have a firm grip. This does not mean the grip of a gorilla, nor does it mean a grip that is so weak that it feels like a wet fish. Accepted business etiquette is a firm handshake that usually goes up and down up two or three times.

Amazingly, so few people are aware of the effect of a proper handshake. Many people have different handshakes and from this, you can gain some insight into their personalities. It is worth practising the proper handshake until it becomes automatic and you don't have to think about it.

Common Handshake Faults

1. Not gripping firmly enough
2. Gripping too firmly to create authority
3. A double-handed "glove" handshake with strangers
4. A finger grab handshake. This is shaking the fingers rather than the hands
5. The dominant handshake, where the arm is fully extended, with the knuckles facing upwards, and the palm facing downwards and thrust towards the individual
6. Not looking at the person while you are shaking hands

If you are meeting with colleagues in a group, make sure that when you shake the person's hand that you state your name and position within the firm or role within it. If meeting the person alone, then this is often accompanied by:

"It's a pleasure to meet you" or, "It's great to meet you."

During the initial meeting, there is a lot of sizing up going on and you will be judged, just as you will be judging. It is important to control the frame and not to be seen to be subservient. Your conduct, the way you look, move, speak, and act, will all convey whether you are a person that someone may wish to talk to and take seriously.

Remembering a Name

There is a special word that people like to hear, and that is their name. Remembering somebody's name is a great rapport builder. I'm sure we have all been in a situation when we have been introduced to somebody and then we have immediately forgotten their name. When someone forgets your name, it can be quite amusing to watch them try to cover this up. They will try to avoid any reference having to use your name.

A story that I still find amusing relates to somebody I know who claimed to have a terrible memory or rather poor recall and decided to do something about it. He bought a book and excitedly called me, explaining that he had bought this fantastic new book to improve his memory. He was raving about it. I was curious to learn more and asked him who had written it, to which he replied:

"Eh, I can't remember!"

Some memory methods can be quite complicated and require practice. A simple method can make things easier. We learn through repetition and can draw on this to help remember names. When somebody first says their name, immediately repeat it with your internal voice. Then repeat their name back to them out loud with an inflection at the end of the sentence, as if asking a question. Finish off by saying: "It's nice to meet you" and then repeat their name.

Let's look at an example of this. Suppose that I meet somebody and his name is Mike. I reach out my hand, introduce myself and say my name:

"Derek, pleased to meet you."

They would then say their name, for example:

"Mike."

As soon as they say their name is Mike, I repeat:

"Mike", inside my head.

I then verbally repeat their name back to them with an inflection, as if asking them a question, and say:

"Mike?"

They would say *"Yes."*

I then say: "Pleased to meet you, Mike."

This allows us time to have heard and repeated their name four times.

The final layer to add to help us remember is to notice if their name reminds us of anything or anyone. Here, we could imagine a large microphone (mic) coming out of Mike's head and create a crazy, illogical image to remember this by. If nothing comes to mind, don't worry, this is just an additional step. If Mike has some particularly prominent feature by linking the microphone to this, will be even more effective. Remember to make the image weird and if you can incorporate sex and violence into the image, so much the better. This will help you remember it! It is your private world and we don't need to tell anyone.

Make the Effort

When meeting people from different countries, particularly if their native language is not English, sometimes their names can be difficult to pronounce and remember. Remember, as we have just discovered, somebody's name is very important to them. Often they may have an English approximation name which we can refer to them by. However, this is not their name! If we can remember their name and try to pronounce it as accurately as we can, this creates a great impression.

Recently I met a woman from Poland named Agnieszka. To pronounce her name properly is difficult for a native English speaker. When she introduced herself, she gave her name and said, "But call me Anna". The "but" was a very important part of the sentence. It meant you can call me Anna because you probably can't pronounce my name! I said to her I would prefer to call her Agnieszka. I repeated her name back to her, asking her if I was pronouncing it correctly and she gave the correct pronunciation. I tried another two times and got the pronunciation close. I then said to her I want to use your proper name, but I may need to ask you occasionally to remind me how to pronounce it properly. This means that if I forget her name rather than saying: *"What is your name again?"*
All I have to say is: "Could you remind me how do you *pronounce* your name again". This presupposes that I can remember it, but the difficulty I'm having is pronouncing it, not remembering it. It's a subtle difference, but language is powerful as we've seen.

Don't Overuse the Name

A word of caution when using somebody's name. Overuse of a name can have a negative effect. If overused, it becomes more of an annoyance than a relationship builder. We often associate this with the stereotypical high-pressure salesperson who realises the importance of somebody's name and yet fails to understand the subtlety of use.

There is not an exact formula of how many times a person's name should be used in a conversation. It should be interspersed naturally. Let's give an example of overusing somebody's name:

"It's great, David, that you have an interest in antiques. Many of our clients have developed a keen interest in the antiques market, David. There are several areas that we could look at, David. Which areas are most appealing to you?"

CHAPTER 19

Getting Conversational

The second stage in a conversation usually revolves around where are you from and what do you do. Something that works well is to use some pacing. Knowing that most people will ask "*What is it that you do?*" and "*Where are you from?*", we can use that to our advantage. By simply saying:

> "*I guess by now I should be asking you what you do. Let's face it, we all have to work, but I'm curious, what is your real passion in life? What is it that drives you and gets you up in the morning?*"

Getting Passionate

When we do this, we are shifting people's awareness away from the world of work and towards pleasure. Once we get people onto topics that someone has a genuine passion or interest in, then we are transporting them to the world of pleasure. If you observe, you will see a change in their facial muscles as they relax and they may even smile more. You have triggered the pleasure of response!

The Family

We have learned the importance of criteria and values and how this establishes the very essence of who people are. It is advisable to tread carefully if asking if somebody has any children. Usually in the conversation, if family ranks high in the priority list, it will be mentioned but it is not always the case, but it is true enough to be true.

In my experience, when speaking to older women, if they have children, showing an interest in their children works well when building rapport. If you can remember their children's names and a bit about them, this works even better. If their daughter has a wedding coming up and you can remember this for the next time you meet them, this generates rapport.

It also work well with some men, too. If there are pictures of the family around, then the family is important. I have noticed that if a man has just recently become a father then they are happy to describe the experience and every intricate detail of the new arrival. Particularly if it is their first child.

Of course, there are exceptions to the rule and we don't want to get involved in stereotypes. These are sweeping generalisations and won't apply to everyone. As communicators, we are just looking for ways to build rapport. If something works, use it. If not, change it. It will depend on the individual and their value set. Your sharpened awareness skills should see you right here.

Borrowed Authority

We looked at the authority principle earlier and the power that it holds. If you are in a position and you don't have authority, a technique that you can use is to "borrow authority". If you are delivering a presentation on which you are not a leading authority, you can borrow the authority of other people by quoting them and their research. This works very well in everyday conversation as long as you are accurate.

Another way to borrow authority is to mention your association with somebody important or something that you have achieved. I would urge caution when using the names of people and places. We don't want to come across as a namedropper. I am sure many of us have come across people like this and it doesn't create a great impression. It is far better if you're borrowing authority to remember to make it targeted and relevant to the point that you are making.

MOVE IT TO THEM

As the conversation develops, we need to have our wits about us and to listen. In the section on state control, we talked about the importance of developing an intense desire to get to know someone and "R+". We also discussed the heart trigger.

We also need to be alert to the changes in body language. Body language patterns in business and everyday life are very different to body language patterns in attraction in seduction. This is such a big topic that the reader is referred to the book by the author "Body Language How to Read Any Body", where it explained in great detail.

At this stage, the aim is to get people talking about themselves. We must remember to show a genuine interest in them through the "question, echo, comment, and question" strategy and that we're not trying to interrogate them.

When I was younger, I remember going out on a date and had just come back from a sales training course where they focused on asking open questions (Chapter 14). I took this too literally and started asking lots of open questions, but I failed to link them together using the "question echo comment question" approach. I remember the girl at the time saying to me, "You ask a lot of questions, don't you!"

This is worth remembering to make asking questions conversational. As you practise this, it will become natural and you won't have to remember the formula.

Enough About Me

Somebody who is an excellent conversationalist will realise that they have been speaking for too long and will want to make sure that the other person gets to speak. If the person you are speaking to asks you a question, remember to not speak for too long. If you feel that you have, a great way to switch the conversation back is to make a joke and say:

"*Anyway, enough about me. I'd like to learn more about....*"

And then return the conversation back.

"And What Do You Do?"

This is one of the most predictable questions that somebody could ask. You almost invariably know that is going to come up in a conversation. This can be a bit of a conversation stopper if not done properly. Before we look at how we can answer this, there is an important principle to be aware of. Your job title is not who you are, it is a state of being. This will become clearer as we go through the example. If someone asks:

"What do you do?"

If you are an accountant, you may reply with

"I'm an accountant."

Now we have already discussed vague language. Informing someone that you're an accountant is quite vague, it doesn't actually say what you do. We want to make what we do sound interesting. Let's see if we can do this again and make it more interesting:

"I specialise in making sure that my clients reduce the amount of unnecessary tax that they pay. I use many special but legal methods to ensure that more of their money is kept by them and their family."

This sounds more interesting than I'm an accountant. It also creates interest and creates an opportunity for the other person to ask questions. Returning to the question comment question process after echoing, we would simply say:

"That sounds fascinating. What type of methods are there that you use?"

We can then ask questions using the "question echo comment question" approach to have a conversation about accountancy about which we know very little.

Conversing When You Know Nothing

One thing that is useful to learn is how to have a conversation about a topic that we know absolutely nothing about. This may seem daunting, but it's very easy. I have had many

164

conversations at length about things that I know absolutely nothing about. We know people like to talk about themselves, particularly if they have expertise in a particular area. All we have to do is ask questions using the "question echo comment question formula". The only thing to be mindful of here is to ask sensible questions. The way we do this is by developing our sharpened awareness skills. Let's look at an example to show this.

I once had a client who was a keen rower. Now, this is something I know absolutely nothing about other than what I've seen from the Olympics. In fairness, it was fun to watch. Let's explore how we can discuss rowing. We can either ask very specific questions or we can ask deeper questions, which gives the person the opportunity to talk more at length. Let's explore this now.

Specific Questions

"What are the boats made of?"

Deeper Questions

"What's the biggest thing that makes for a successful rowing team?"

All we have to do is to keep asking questions and we can vary them between specific and deeper questions. The key here is to use the "R+" technique and develop a curiosity together with the "question, echo, comment, question" method.

Behind the Scenes

One way that we can enhance our communication skills when we speak is to build a journal of knowledge. As you become older, you will have more life experiences to draw upon. If you are younger and have had as little experience, simply borrow other people's experiences and stories and use them when you speak. It's very useful to have a notebook or a journal where you can write interesting pieces of information or quotes that you like. For example, one of my favourite quotes is from Henry Ford:

> *"Whether you think that you can or think that you can't you're right."*

There is someone I know who when he was younger used to have a joke book. In this book, he would write all his favourite jokes and he used to rehearse before he went out on a date. Now I'm not advocating that this is the best way to impress a date. I would suggest that this is not the best way to do it. However, the principle is correct, which is to have things that are amusing or stories that you can draw on and fit in with the conversation. We are not delivering a stand-up routine!

What's in the Papers?

It's always worthwhile checking what is going on in the world by either having a glance at the newspapers or going online and checking various news channels. It is worth looking at several news channels to make sure that you get different perspectives. If a major event has happened and you're not aware of it, this dents your credibility. I remember when I was with a colleague and a client of mine asked a question relating to a major event. My colleague looked at him blankly and my client said:

> *"Where have you been for the last two weeks, on the moon?"*

Industry Knowledge

If you are meeting people either in a specific industry or who have a specific interest, it is worthwhile doing some basic research beforehand. If you know that there is a hot topic that is affecting their industry or their interests, mentioning this will gain you massive rapport. Just as in the example, with rowing you don't have to be an expert, all you have to do is to ask questions. If you are meeting with a business and you can refer to their flagship product or a new product launch during your conversation, this will show interest and that you have bothered to have done some research.

If you know that you are going to be speaking to a particular individual, then doing some background checking on their social media profile, website or any blogs will give you information that you can refer to. It's very flattering when someone can refer to something about you. For example, if someone met me and said: " I've read one of your books, you can imagine the effect this has on rapport building". The way to make this comment more effective is to add some extra information. For example, if somebody said to me: "I've read your book, and I loved the chapter on questions" that says to me they have shown an interest but also that they have read the book or at least given the impression of reading the book.

Be very careful about contacting people and doing no research. I have people contacting me via social media, probably by an automated bot mentioning dealing with businesswomen like me and asking if I have ever thought of writing a book!

Stroke Feathers or Fur

Everybody likes to have their feathers or their fur stroked. I don't mean this literally. What I'm referring to is that everybody likes to be acknowledged and recognised for what they have done. When you are asking somebody a question and show an interest and ask them to tell you more, particularly if it is something that they are proud of, they will usually respond.

Nothing is "Nice"

When we're wanting to build rapport with people and pay them compliments, people are often very unimaginative when using descriptive words. How many times have we heard "that's a nice jacket" or "you have a nice car". This word trip off the tongue too easily and gives the impression of not having put any thought into the compliment. Remember, people, respond better if you say something and then give a reason. Let's look at a couple of examples:

"I really love the colour and style of your jacket."

"Your new car has beautiful lines, I've always admired that make and model."

These descriptions sound much better than you have a nice car and you have a nice jacket. Remember to put some effort into making a compliment and give a reason as to why you like something.

Conversation Linkers

We have discovered the very simple technique called "question echo comment question" and yet some of us struggle when it comes to the comment part. The best way is to develop a genuine interest in what the person is saying and be curious to find out more. Let's look at some phrases that we can use to help us:

"That sounds fascinating I've always wanted to know how....."

"How interesting, how did you first learn how to.....?"

"That's amazing, I'm curious when did you first discover?"

"I would never have known that, where did you find....?"

There are many more, of course, and you can use the ones that fit best with the country and culture that you are in. A good idea is to write some of these down. The very act of writing things down has the effect of cementing them in your mind. This also means that you can glance at these periodically until they become unconsciously embedded.

Are You Welcome?

If you are approaching two people who are standing facing each other and in discussion and their body language does not open up when you approach, this could indicate that you are not invited to join in.

How Are You?

When we meet people, one of the first questions is:

"How are you?"

At this point, it is not a good idea to start complaining. Everybody has their cross to bear. If things are going well, be aware that even though people may be pleased for you, part of them that is envious. The reason for this is that it highlights the parts of their life that are not. If things are going very well for you, it's always better to admit to a small challenge first before delivering the good news. An example will make this clearer:

"We had a really tough time at the beginning of the year attracting new customers and hitting our targets, but

recently things have turned around and are looking positive for us."

This gives a more balanced approach. Nobody likes people who boast and who continually tell everyone how much money they are making and how successful they are. I know a couple of people who are like this and they complain they don't have any friends.

It's Time to Party

I have always found parties to be an interesting dynamic. There are two main scenarios.
1. Standing up and mingling
2. Sitting down at a table

When people go to a party and they're standing up and mingling, you can observe some interesting behaviour. Many people, when speaking to others, will be continually looking around the room almost as if to see if they're missing out on anything. Perhaps it may be to see if there is anybody more interesting or more attractive they should be speaking to. Be very careful if you do this, as it is very off-putting for the listener. If you do spot somebody that you want to speak to, you can make your excuses to break the conversation. A bathroom break usually does the trick with this.

If you are at a party and you're in a seated environment or at a table, it is harder to get up and leave. It also presents an additional challenge of trying to speak to people on both sides and the person opposite as well. It is worth sharpening your awareness skills and noticing if anybody is feeling left out and to engage in a conversation with them. Be careful of the usual expected questions, "What do you do? and "Where are you from?"

The No Go Areas

There are certain areas that it is best to avoid unless you know that somebody has the same opinions as you. It is also worth being careful about presuming somebody's viewpoint. It may not be as predicted. We want to sort for sameness and not for difference.

The main areas that are worth avoiding are:

1. Religion
2. Politics
3. Political movements/causes
4. Health
5. Money
6. Gossip
7. Criticising somebody
8. Death
9. Sex
10. Inappropriate humour

Say No Evil

A good principle to adopt is to avoid speaking "ill about people". This is very much the case if you're meeting somebody for the first time or that you don't know well. If you talk "ill of somebody", assume that it will get back to them.

Some people enjoy gossip and will try to draw you in to speak ill about another person. It is wise to resist this temptation, irrespective of how much we agree with them.

I remember once when I first started my career in sales, and being in a client's office when he took a telephone call. He was extremely pleasant to the person on the call and was very engaging. However, as soon as he ended the call and put the phone down, he immediately said what an idiot the person was and even gave me their name. I was a bit shocked by this. Later that day, when speaking to a good friend of mine who also used to meet him in a sales capacity, I mentioned I had had an unusual meeting with this client. He mentioned to me he had the same experience. I remember thinking that if this client is speaking ill of other people, what is he saying about me after a phone call.

A great way to get out of speaking ill of somebody else when somebody is trying to draw you in is to use the lack of knowledge trick. We simply say:

"I don't know them that well or I haven't seen them recently, so I'm not sure what they've been up to."

Then you can change the subtly change the subject.

Phone Smile

A technique that works very well when you're speaking to people on the phone is to smile when you're speaking. As there is a link between the mind body connection, the act of smiling will then make your voice congruent and sound more appealing on the phone.

CHAPTER 20

Captivation Secrets

As the conversation develops and we hear the person speak, this gives us more clues on how to develop rapport using our voice. There are many things that we can identify in someone's voice.

1. Energy and excitement
2. Pace
3. Volume
4. Accent
5. Timbre
6. Expression
7. Tone
8. Intonation
9. Type of words

We know we reflect thoughts in the outer expression. This occurs with people's voices as too. Extroverts have louder and more expressive voices and speak quickly, often changing the subject, and having poor attention spans. We can gain clues into somebody's inner world by looking at those variables listed above. We may notice that somebody uses a word in conversation a bit like a catchphrase. I remember being on a webinar once, where one particular individual explained how he taught people to be better public speakers. He was blissfully unaware of the number of times that he said, "in essence". Once I was aware of this, it was very difficult to concentrate on what he was saying, as he was using it so often.

By paying attention and realising that this is a catchphrase of his, if we were to incorporate this into our dialogue with him it would create rapport at an unconscious level.

SPEAKING CONFIDENTLY

Sounding Intelligent

Some of the best communicators have a great command of the English language. Their skill lies in knowing when to use an extended vocabulary and when to use everyday words.

If you have an extended vocabulary, simply using one or two lesser used words when speaking creates the impression that you are well read and intelligent. This does not mean reciting the dictionary. However, being able to use words with a specific meaning will gain credibility with other people. The easy way to do this is to read classic books and when you see a word that you're not familiar with, write it down and look up the definition.

Think about the new word that you discover. Is this a word that you could incorporate into your communication? For example, "prognostication" while being a great word is not one that we would hear, whereas "verbose" would be one that we could use. I would urge caution when using lesser known words with somebody of a limited vocabulary. We don't want to come across as pompous and to make people feel uneasy, but equally, if we meet somebody with a large vocabulary, it is useful to inject a few less popular words into our communication.

Two words that I like are "verbose" (uses many words to say something) and "obsequious" (paying an undue amount of respect) as we can use both these words when communicating. I am careful when using those words as many people don't know the meaning of them and we don't want to make people feel uncomfortable.

Watch the Tone

People spend too much time focusing on the content of what they are speaking about and not enough time on how they deliver the message. People will forget what we said, but they will never forget how we made them feel. We have discussed state control and body position earlier and how important it is.

When we are speaking, we must control our speed and not speak too quickly. Pay attention to any inflection that we may have in our voice. It's often easy to spot a native Latin language speaker such as French, Spanish or Italian when they speak English. In their native language, one way to ask a question is to make a statement and have a rising tone at the end of the sentence. In English, we always have a question word before we ask a question. If we make a statement with a rising tone, it can show uncertainty or a question.

I have observed that in some parts of the USA and parts of Glasgow in Scotland, some people have a rising tone at the end of their sentence. This gives the impression of showing less conviction.

Tone it Down

Imagine that you were standing in a room and suddenly there was an object flying towards you. If I shouted:

"Get Down!"

How would it sound? It would be loud, but the tone would go down at the end of the sentence. A tone that goes down at the end of the sentence indicates a command. If you want to make an important point in a conversation or when you are delivering a presentation or when public speaking, be aware of the different tonalities.

Add Some Expression

One of the key ways to add expression to the topic that you are discussing is to get passionate about it. This involves the voice rising and falling in a natural rhythm. This is harder to do than you may think.

When I have been coaching people, I have asked them to describe something in their normal tone. I have then asked them to add some expression to this. When we have been recording these sessions and they hear the playback, there is a negligible difference. If you want to add expression, you *really, really* have to exaggerate this for it to have any noticeable effect.

If not convinced, record yourself and see what I mean. If you're not feeling uncomfortable and felt that you have perhaps over exaggerated your delivery, then it probably won't even be noticed by the other person.

A great way to practise this is to pick up a magazine or a book and read a paragraph in your normal voice tonality. Record this on your mobile phone or a recording device and then repeat this, but this time add expression. When you do this, you will realise how much you have to exaggerate to get any expression at all. You need to practise this and again state control comes into play. Somebody who has a wonderful rhythm and lilt to his voice together with adding wonderful expression is the Scottish comedian Billy Connolly.

Analogue Marking

An advanced technique that you can use when speaking to people and wanting to be persuasive is called vocal analogue marking. This involves emphasising and marking certain parts of your message. Marking can be done in several ways. Let's look at two simple ways that you can do this.

Vocal Marking

When using our voice to engage in vocal analogue marking we emphasise certain words. One of the easiest ways to do this is simply to have a longer pause before delivering our key point. When delivering our key point, we need to make sure that the voice intonation is flat and if it is a command that it goes down. Let's look at an example to illustrate this:

"As we are learning to enhance our communication skills from reading this book, it is important that we remember to.........." (Pause) "read this more than once!" (Command tone)

Another way to use analogue marking is to use your arm to emphasise the words either in a chopping action or in a drumming action. You can further enhance this by nodding your head at the same time as analogue marking with your arm. You can combine this by using a pause for even greater effect. We can also use one hand to emphasise good news and the other hand to emphasise bad news:

"On one hand we have.........and on the other hand we have....."

Don't be too concerned if this seems complicated as this is an advanced skill and comes with practise. You can communicate very effectively without it.

Show You Are Listening

As we discussed earlier, the most important words that a person hears are the ones that they have just spoken. It is very important that we not only listen, but that we show we are listening as well. There are three methods to do this which are very simple and are very effective.

1. The first one is to tilt your head about 30 degrees to one side. For examples, please consult the book <u>Body Language How to Read Any Body.</u>
2. The second method is to nod your head periodically. This shows the person at an unconscious level that you agree with what they're saying.
3. The third way to show that you are listening is to use words and expressions like "fascinating", "how interesting", "uh huh", "right", "okay".

Nobody likes to feel that they're not being listened to. Have you ever had a call from somebody who is on their mobile or cell phone and they're doing something else while they are speaking to you and you have to say to them:

"Can you hear me? Are you still there?"

Match the Energy

When speaking to people, we must measure the energy level and position our energy accordingly. There is nothing worse than a mismatch in energy. While having the energy of a game show host may be suitable for television, it would hardly be appropriate if you're speaking to somebody at a funeral. My opinion is that it is better to raise your energy a little more than the person or the group that you're talking to and then gradually raise this as you are speaking to them. Equally, if you meet somebody who has a high energy level and is enthusiastic, speaking to them as if you are at a funeral is unlikely to generate any rapport.

Pointing and Getting Closer

It is good to be aware of some basic body language patterns. The feet and the legs are the most honest part of the body. They are the part that we have the least control of and the part that we are least aware of. The feet will always point in the direction of someone who we are attracted to or who is dominant in the group.

If you see somebody's feet pointing in a different direction when you're speaking, it is a sure sign that the conversation is ending. If you see both feet pointing in that direction with the torso turned around, it is time to wrap up the conversation quickly.

We discussed the principle of outward expression reflecting inner thought. If we are interested in somebody and like what they're saying, we will naturally be closer to them. One thing to watch for is people moving closer towards you. This is often subtle. If somebody moves away or leans back, it could indicate that they don't like what you're saying and wish to move away.

Cultural Differences

If you are want to build rapport with somebody and to connect with them, it is important to be aware of different cultures, expressions and use of words that can occur in English. Let's look at a couple of examples of these.

If you are from the UK and you're speaking to somebody from the USA, it is worth bearing in mind that there are language differences and to use the other person's words whenever possible. For example, use:

1. Elevator instead of lift
2. Sidewalk instead of pavement
3. February 25th instead of the 25th of February
4. Bathroom instead of toilet
5. Vacation instead of holiday

The list goes on and a sharpened awareness and making a note of when you hear differences and learning them will help build rapport.

I want to share an amusing story with you about how a lack of awareness of the difference in the language can sometimes have an embarrassing effect. There was a European sales conference in Vienna, in Austria. I was working for a large American company at the time and the chief executive had flown over and was due to give her speech.

She came to the podium in a room filled with over five hundred people. She wasn't sure of the dress code and what she should wear in Europe and, as an icebreaker, she announced:

"I didn't know if I should wear pants or not."

If you are reading this and you're from the US, this will seem perfectly normal. However, if you are reading this and you are outside North America and you are in Europe then you may have had a small chuckle to yourself.

In British English, pants mean underwear. In British English, the word for pants is trousers. The chief executive of this large American company had just stated to the European audience that she didn't know whether she should wear any underwear. There was a lot of chuckling going on and she was unaware of the joke. Puzzled by the laughing, she asked a colleague from the UK what was going on. She then learned the meaning of "pants" in Europe. It was rather amusing, and she took it in good spirit.

Cultural Behaviour

Cultural differences and etiquette are big topics and if you are travelling a lot, it is worth learning about the differences to make sure that you don't make a big mistake. I have found from my travels around Europe and when visiting more remote locations that the more remote a place is, they place more emphasis on people getting to know one another.

I was lucky enough to go to the Mediterranean island of Malta regularly on business. If you haven't visited Malta, I would highly recommend it. It is beautiful and the people are friendly. I quickly established that doing business in Malta was very different from doing business in the UK. It was a much softer approach, and people wanted to get to know you. On a couple of occasions, I was invited to meet with clients' families at a celebration dinner and a barbecue. It was all about building trust and getting to know each other. When working in bigger cities, it becomes less personal. It is always worthwhile having a general knowledge of as many places as we can so that if we meet somebody and discover that they're from a particular place, then you can refer to it.

Just as there are cultural differences in the US, the same holds for Europe. To illustrate some differences that exist between different countries in Europe, I'm going to share an amusing story with you.

I was at a European sales conference in continental Europe while working for a large American company. All the European country's offices were gathered together for this large conference. The company liked to mix up the seating over dinner so that people from different countries were seated together. At the table where I was sitting, there were people from Austria, France, Spain, Scandinavia and the UK. After dinner, the conversation turned to saunas and the health benefits. Somebody at the table mentioned they enjoyed going to a sauna but discovered that when they went to Austria that they had to remove all of their clothing. On learning about this, the French people started shaking their heads disapprovingly. In response, a man from Austria said I don't know what is wrong with this. It's perfectly natural, and it's more hygienic to remove your clothing. He then explained how he took his top client, a buyer from a car manufacturer, regularly to a sauna where they would discuss business and she loved it. A man from the UK then interrupted and tried to be funny and said:

"You kinky devil!"

This did not go down well with our Austrian colleagues. This just goes to show we all have our maps of the world and we must meet people at their level of reality.

Language Fillers

Think about confident people. How do they sound? Their voices are confident, relaxed and they have very few "ahs", "ehs" or "ums", when they speak. They have a tone that does down at the end of the sentence. Let's have a look now at unnecessary fillers.

A big giveaway that you are nervous is the use of "ahs", "ehs" and "ums". Many people struggle with this and yet it is very easy to sort these unwanted fillers. Whenever you feel you want to say an "eh", "ah", or "um" just simply slow down and take a pause. This takes a bit of practise. The easiest way to do this is to put your phone down in front of you and start recording and simply talk about anything that you want. It will soon become apparent if there are many "ehs", "ahs", and "ums". Whenever you feel the need for any "ehs", "ahs", and "ums" simply take a pause. It's easy to correct.

The next thing to avoid is what I call "language fillers" these are unnecessary words. In the UK a common thing that I have observed is hearing a waiter or waitress adding unnecessary language when asking a question. For example:

"Would you like any water for the table....at all?"

The at all usually fades off at the end of the sentence in a weak voice and is a sure sign that the person is not confident. If you do this, make a mental note of it and correct it next time. You can practise this by making statements that go down at the end of the sentence and stopping the sentence abruptly. This avoids the temptation to add on unnecessary language fillers. Another variation of this is adding the word "no" at the end of the sentence. For example:

"Perhaps we could meet tomorrow and go to the cinema.....no?"

The Big Pause

This is one of the most powerful things that you can use aside from the proper use of questions to gain people's interest and to hold their attention. Imagine that we are walking down the street in our own little world and suddenly there is a loud sound that frightens us. Immediately, we come back to full awareness. This is called a pattern interrupt.

The same thing occurs when speaking to somebody. They expect us to speak in a certain way and at a certain pace. If you suddenly stop speaking, this is not as predicted in the brain's model and people come back to full awareness wondering what is going on.

I have used this frequently and trained people extensively on this technique. Next time when you're speaking to somebody, just simply insert a long pause and I mean a long pause and watch how their eye contact immediately comes to you and you have their full attention. The only challenge we have when learning this is that most people feel uncomfortable inserting a pause and they don't insert a long enough one. To practise, use a mobile or cell phone and press the record button and start speaking. You can talk about anything you want and then just insert a long pause. Play it back and if you are like most people, you may find that the pause is hardly detectable. In the same way that we have to exaggerate our expression for it to be noticed, we have to do the same with the pause. If the pause is not feeling uncomfortable, then the chances are that it is not long enough. This is a great technique to get people's attention back. It's useful if you're delivering a presentation, speaking to a group of people and in a one-to-one situation where you detect someone's attention has drifted.

Measuring Engagement

Typical signs of engagement in a conversation include:

1. Nodding
2. Smiling
3. Laughing
4. Eye contact
5. Longer answers to your questions
6. Giving more detail when answering
7. Moving closer to you and leaning in
8. Asking questions
9. Relaxation of the facial muscles
10. A fuller and redder lower lip
11. Relaxation of the body

How to Engage a Group

Engaging with the group requires a unique skill set. Once you develop your confidence and know that speaking is something that you can do without thinking, then this allows more of your conscious mind to observe people and their actions. When you see a group of people, it's worth paying attention to the tenseness that they are showing on their bodies and faces. When I see overly tense people, it alerts me they may be problematic. It's always good to identify a friendly, relaxed person in the group to connect with.

One of the big mistakes that people make when speaking to groups of people is that they just speak to one person, and this makes others feel left out. If we are speaking to a group of people, particularly if we are presenting, then we must make eye contact with everybody in the group. A great way to get people involved is to link the conversation and just ask the next person in the group:

> *"That's a great point, Sue. What are your thoughts on this, John?"*

You can practise this in a social environment with groups of friends and it is very easy to do. The key thing is to have an open and friendly demeanour and to be playful. Many charismatic people use humour and are playful in their approach.

If running a meeting for a group of people or hosting a video conference, make sure everybody gets involved. If people are introverted and don't like speaking, a great way to get them involved is to "stroke their fur". We do this by acknowledging their competence in a particular area or a skill set that they have and then ask them for their opinion.

Let's suppose that we were in a group conversation in a business environment. Let's assume that we were want to replace our existing IT system with a new IT system. The people in the online meeting come from different parts of the business. Within that group, there will be a few that will be experts and there will be others that will know less about it and may be reluctant to contribute. When running a meeting, we must make sure that we include as many people as possible. If you identify somebody who is more introverted and who is quieter, an easy way to get them involved is to say:

> *"Sarah, I know that you have experience of moving from one system to another in the past. What are some of the issues that you think we should be aware of?"*

If it is someone is an expert in the area but is quiet and reluctant to get involved, an easy thing to say is:

"Chris, I know that this is an expertise of yours and we would all value your opinion."

Group Social Gathering

Some useful phrases to use when entering a group are:

"This looks like where it is all happening"

"So, this is where all the fun people hang out?"

"So, how do you all know each other?"

CHAPTER 21

Using Questions for Power

We can also use questions to gain control, change reality, and create credibility. The poor use of questions is one of the biggest mistakes that I see in communication and yet this is a simple thing to fix. Knowing how to use questions properly not only enables you to get the information that you want, but it also enables you to gain control and to have more power. In any communication, people will attach their own meaning. Questions are a useful way to clarify meaning and also to gain control over any conversation, meeting, presentation, or speech.

Voltaire understood the power of questions and another favourite quote of mine is:

"Judge a man by his questions rather than by his answers."

This is a very profound statement. Having the ability to ask the correct questions not only enhances your credibility but also gives the impression of being a thinker and being interested.

QUESTION RULES

Big Rule No. 1

"People in power ask questions and those not in power answer them."

Think about who asks you questions, policemen, judges, your boss, etc. If we adopt the position of the questioner rather than the answerer, then this enables us to gain power and to give time to think.

Big Rule No. 2

"Do not answer any question until you understand what the question is about"

When somebody asks a question, very often people assume we know what information is being asked for. This can cause people to give away too much information or irrelevant information and get themselves in bother. Let's look at an example of this. Suppose that you work in project management and your boss has summoned you to give an update on the project. Your boss may say:

"I'm not happy with the way this project is being run. It seems like a shambles. What is going on?"

What does a shambles mean? It is an adjective and is subjective and relative. The boss' real meaning behind the question may have been:

"Why have I not been given progress reports?"

Don't volunteer any information until you fully understand the question.

Big Rule Number 3

"Most people don't know what they are talking about at a deeper level."

Most people have a surface knowledge of things. If you ask questions and probe deeper, this becomes apparent quickly. It takes only a few questions before someone is exposed. This is a powerful technique.

Be careful if doing this, as we don't want to make people look silly. We just want clarity but equally, we also don't want resistance or a breakdown in rapport. Language softeners will help you here.

The Summary

A great method to ensure understanding is to summarise:

"Just to check my understanding, your main concern is the lack of communication and regular reports. If I supply you with a weekly update of progress, is that what you are looking for?"

The Finale

Finishing up by saying:

"Does that answer your question?"

This will allow you to make sure that you have a mutual understanding and that you have addressed all the issues.

QUESTIONS TO APPLY PRESSURE

I'm going to share with you one of the most powerful techniques that you can use in any situation. It involves a sharpening of awareness and really paying attention to what is being said and using questions. Many people speak in generalisations and they use adjectives and adverbs which have no meaning other than the meaning that someone attaches to them. If I said:

"The car was driving slowly."

What does that actually mean? Let's look at a power display example and will use a work situation for this. Imagine that we wanted to put somebody under pressure or perhaps we want people to give us more information than they otherwise would. The technique here is to use very general questions. Let's imagine that there is a manager who wants to put someone in his team under pressure and to find out as much information as he can. The manager can ask a very general question and see what information comes back. For example:

"I'm very unhappy with the way this project is being run. It seems to be chaotic. What's going on?"

Let's suppose that the response was:

"We've had a lot of problems with the team. John just hasn't been delivering for the team. Finance has not approved the budget for the developments that we're looking for. We have had staff sickness problems and part of the IT system has not been integrated into the project."

Think about the answer been given. A lot of information has been volunteered to a general, non-specific question. This can be very dangerous. Let's look at the question now.

The person who asked it is unhappy. However, what *exactly* are they unhappy about and what *exactly* seems to be chaotic? Now, if you are in a senior position and want to put somebody under pressure, this is a great technique, as you're giving people enough of an opportunity to incriminate themselves.

If you get asked a question like that, be very careful before answering it. We don't know what the question is about. In this situation, it is far better to get the person to be more specific about what they're looking for. We need to draw on the skills that we've learned previously to make this more effective. If you simply say:

"What do you mean chaotic?"

This can come across as being confrontational. A better way to do this is to use some language softeners, echo, frame and pace before you ask your question. We could say:

"This project is a big project and there are many moving parts (softener and pace) and in order not to waste your time (pre frame), which parts of the project are you unhappy with that seemed to be chaotic?"(echoing)

We have now put the ball back into the manager's court and put the pressure on him to clarify what he means. We may discover that the only part that he is concerned with is that he feels that the reporting has not been clear enough and he doesn't know what is going on. This saves us from having to volunteer information that he may not have been aware of.

By giving a reply like that, to the manager, we have turned the pressure back. The way for the manager to avoid being drawn in is for him to avoid being specific and to be general and vague again:

"Sarah, as you are the project manager and responsible for the project, I would have expected you to have known that this project is chaotic."

The pressure has now been turned again. We just use the same technique as before. This time, if we detect that there is more frustration in his voice, we can pace this in our reply. We can also insert some fairness into our reply. Let's have a look at an example:

"As the project manager for the project (echo) I can understand your frustration with the project (pace). I want to make sure that you have all the information that you need (pre frame). I know that you are pushed for time (pace and giving a reason), I wonder if you would be able to (language softener), highlight your main (narrowing down) concern.

This takes practise and the best time to practise is not in front of your boss or someone in authority. When I am coaching people, we do extensive role plays where I will put people under pressure to encourage them to practise this technique.

The first step is to identify that somebody is speaking using vague language is to listen and pay attention to adjectives and adverbs. When asking clarifying questions, we must ask in the correct manner. Our state control will help us here. A poorly phrased question delivered with the right intent can still get excellent results.

CHAPTER 22

Dealing with Challenging People

We have all met people who are challenging, difficult, or just plain awkward. Wouldn't the world be a lot better if everyone was just more like us? We know they have their map of the world and they don't think they are difficult. We need some techniques that we can use when speaking to them.

Aggressive or Forceful Individuals

Many of us have come across people who are forceful or aggressive. There is a technique we can use which involves using nonverbal communication. If someone is becoming too forceful or is verbally attacking you, simply raising your hand in the stop sign will be picked up unconsciously. The stop sign is universally recognised. This does not mean raising your hand and putting it in front of their face. If you're speaking to them while standing up, simply raise your hand to your side to show the stop sign. If you're sitting at a desk, you can raise your hand from the desk.

The Complainers

A great way to deal with complainers who are not happy is just to agree with them. For an argument to take place, there have to be two opposing points of view.

"I want to complain about the service. No one returns my calls. I have emailed several times and no one replies. It is absolutely disgraceful and I am very angry!"

We just have to agree with them and then use the word "and" with the solution:

"I agree with you, (agreement) the service has been absolutely disgraceful (echoing) and if I were you, I would be very angry too (agreement and echoing). It is not acceptable that no one has returned your calls and replied to your emails (echoing and pacing) AND that is why I am calling you to sort this problem out and to make sure that you are happy"

Someone who is very angry may have another rant, but it is very difficult to argue with someone who agrees with you and who echoes and paces you. The rant will often fizzle out quickly. They often may even apologise for their frustration.

Getting a Word In

Some people just don't know when to be quiet. We covered earlier that it is important not to interrupt people. However, some people go on and on for such a long time that it is hard to speak. If you are in a sales or business environment, it's all very well listening to people, but you have to communicate your message. I remember one person who used to talk at me for about two hours and would always complain about how busy they were!

There is a very useful technique that we can use here. We link what they've said to what we want to say and just use the word "and". I would urge caution when using this technique, as you are hijacking the conversation. However, sometimes, it is necessary as some people have such low self-awareness. They are unaware of the rules of communication and engagement and that it should be taken in turns. An example will make this clearer.

Let's assume that the person is in full flow and we are looking for an opportunity to interject without appearing rude. This is how we can do it. Let's assume that they are saying:

"The problem with many businesses these days is that they just don't invest properly in themselves to grow their business to get more customers and to really dominate the market....."

At this point, there is an opportunity for us to interject. All we have to do is use the word "and", then link this to what we want to talk about:

".....and I totally agree with you and that's exactly why we have developed this proprietary IT system that can help segment customers in a new way to target them and help businesses get more customers and to dominate the market"

Notice in that sentence we have agreed with them, which makes the hijacking of their sentence feel less intrusive, and then we have echoed what they have said in the latter part of the sentence.

Getting Away From Boring People

I'm sure we've all had the experience of being in the company of somebody where the conversation is heavy going or we have been trapped and not been able to speak to somebody that we wanted to. There are techniques we can use to get away from people without offending someone. If speaking at an event or presenting, we can simply say to people:

"Could you excuse me for one minute, please? I need to check that all my literature has been set out properly?"

"Could you excuse me one second please, I need to visit the bathroom?"

"Could you excuse me one second please, I have a message on my phone? I'm expecting a call from my partner that I need to take."

When doing this make sure that you move to another room or go to the bathroom. Don't just simply walk a few yards or metres and start speaking to somebody else.

Agreeing without Agreeing

When we are communicating with people, we are looking for similarities and not differences. It is impossible to be identical to the other person and there will be things we may not agree on. This can be quite difficult, particularly if it is a political or social viewpoint that the other person has that you feel strongly against. Let's use an example.

Imagine that you are in the United States of America, and let's suppose that you are very much in favour of people being able to bear arms and have guns. Let's suppose that the person you're speaking to vehemently opposes this and thinks that we should remove guns from everyone. This is tricky because if you agree with them, then you're sacrificing your principles, and if you disagree with them, then you risk losing any rapport that you had previously built.

There is a very clever technique that you can use to avoid this conflict and still hold your views. Imagine that, the person said:

"There are far too many guns around and something needs to be done about the gun situation."

The way to answer this is by being artfully vague:

"Yes guns definitely need to be discussed."

Most people will attach the meaning that they want to a sentence. If you read that again carefully, you will see that I have not agreed to get rid of guns, but I have agreed that they need to be discussed. Skilled communicators use this technique and it allows people to attach their meaning and interpretation to what you say. It is powerful when vague language is used. People that have a sharpened awareness may pick up on this and say:

"We don't need to discuss this. We need to take action!"

If this happens, try one more vague statement and then look to change the subject:

"Yes, nothing happens without action!"

If you feel the conversation slipping away from you, try using a distraction technique. You can either do this physically, by dropping something or by verbally changing the subject. If you try to change the subject too abruptly, the person will know. A great way to do this is to pat the front of your head with your hand and say:

"I've just remembered I was supposed to ask you about..."

Or we can say:

"I'm sorry, I just remembered that I need to phone my dentist about an appointment"

People Who Can't Play Tennis

Some people don't realise that a conversation is a two way thing. We don't play tennis on one side of the court. Ideally, there should be questions from both sides. There is one individual that I know who is very challenging. They never ask any questions. This can be quite difficult. Even when you give them "a hook" by mentioning something for them to ask a question about, they still don't pick up on it. Sometimes you can't win them all! Please, just ask someone a question even if it is just one. They will appreciate it.

A Challenging Audience Member

If you have ever done any presenting or public speaking one thing at the back of your mind, is hoping that there won't be any awkward people in the audience or troublesome questions.

Over the years, I have delivered thousands of presentations. I remember being filled with dread when I looked at the guest list in one particular city to see that one of the most awkward people that I've ever come across had registered to attend. I had experienced this individual over many years and had to handle many complaints, none of which had any grounds and were designed to cause inconvenience to people. When I saw his name on the list, I was dismayed. A colleague of mine informed me not to worry as he always registers but never turns up. On this occasion, however, he did!

True to form, as the presentation started, his aim was to ruin the presentation and be as disruptive as possible and to make the presenters of which I was one look as foolish as possible. During the presentation, he continually nudged his secretary disapprovingly.

As we approached question time, his hand shot up in the air like a man possessed, desperate to ask a question. He had spotted a small anomaly on one slide and was using this as an opportunity to hijack the presentation and make us look foolish. He kept asking more and more petty questions, and as he did so, I noticed that the audience was becoming restless. Many were looking quite frustrated. It was at this moment that I had a moment of inspiration. As he asked another question, I then addressed the rest of the audience. "What does everyone else think?" A man leaned over to him and said:

"Can you be quiet, please, and let them get on with the presentation? I want to listen to what they have to say and you're disrupting it!"

This is a great technique to use if you have somebody who is being awkward, particularly if you sense that other people in the group are aware of this too. By simply turning the question back to the group, they can do the work for you. I have used this technique several times, and it works extremely well.

CHAPTER 23

Story Time

After state control and rapport, telling stories are the next most powerful thing to use if you want to influence somebody. All persuasive and charismatic people use effective stories, either consciously or unconsciously. Stories allow people to conclude what you want them to. The six most powerful words in history are:

"Let me tell you a story"

Storytelling is a big topic and in this chapter, we're going to focus on practical ways that you can use a story when you are communicating, presenting or speaking.

Neural Coupling

Science has shown that neural coupling takes place when storytelling occurs. Neuroscientist Uri Hasson has used functional magnetic resonance imaging (fMRI) from his lab to reveal that our brains show similar activity when we both hear the same story. Once the story starts, our brain activity becomes synced, or what Hasson calls "aligned". The results show that during successful communication, the speaker's and listener's brains exhibit joint, temporally coupled response patterns.

Toronto Neuroscientist Endel Tulving found that the areas of the brain that we use for memory and imagination are identical. Our brains cannot distinguish between the two. Stories are a way to connect an unknown future to a known experience.

Death by PowerPoint

I am sure many of us have listened to (and suffered through) long PowerPoint presentations made up of bullet points, small font size, and confusing information that bores us all. Even if the presenter is animated, we think in pictures and dull bullet points are hard to create a picture of and consequently, we often drift off.

When a story is used to convey facts, things occur in the brain. It's not just the language processing parts in our brain that are activated, but other areas in our brain that we would use when experiencing the events of the story that are activated too. Action words, like drive, engage the motor cortex, leading to a more connected and richer experience of the message.

If a speaker uses stories to impart information, then the listener's experience and understanding will be closer to what the speaker intended. Think about horror stories. Our heart rate increases, we get Goosebumps and the hairs on the back of our necks stand on end. Stories allow us to experience and simulate an event without having to experience it. According to Princeton neuroscientist Uri Hasson, stories activate parts in the brain, and the listener turns the story into their idea and experience. This gives us a better understanding and perspective of the world.

Think about how we communicate as human beings. If we go to a bar or a restaurant with a friend, we don't sit down and quote facts at each other. Could you imagine telling somebody the tallest mountain in Great Britain is Ben Nevis with a height of 4,413 ft. or 1,345 metres and the average rainfall in New York City is 2.456 inches or 618.4 mm or that the hottest month in Toronto in Canada is July 21°C (70°F). Many of us would find this behaviour unusual and it would become boring after a while. Our imagination has little to do and will not be engaged. We tell stories as part of our everyday life with our friends and family, so why do we insist on conveying facts when we are speaking to strangers or communicating in a business environment. When we hear a story, we attach our meaning to that story.

Adverbs and adjectives are very vague words and don't have any specific meaning. The meaning is relative. Let's look at an example. If I said:

> *"I went for a walk and saw a man walking slowly down the street."*

What does that actually mean? It has a different meaning for different people. Slowly is a purely subjective word. It is an adverb and we attach our own meaning to it. To attach meaning to a vague sentence, the brain conducts a transderivational search in which it attempts to attach meaning to vague communication. This requires brainpower and while a person is doing this, they drift into their internal world to make sense of the meaning. Remember that when we are communicating, if we are using vague language such as adjectives and adverbs, then people will attach a subjective meaning to this. If I said I saw a man walking at 2 mph or 2.4 kph, this leaves little to interpret, as it is a statement of fact. It's no coincidence that poetry and fiction novels use a lot of adjectives and adverbs to get people's imagination engaged.

It is a key point to remember that when we want to communicate facts to be as specific as possible and use adjectives and adverbs when we want people to imagine things.

Relevant

When constructing our story, make sure that the story applies to the audience. For the audience to understand the story, they have to put themselves in that position. If you are speaking to a group of retired people and you use a story relating to a current pop star, then the story will not resonate with them. They cannot identify with the character. This is obvious, but I have seen people use stories before where they just do not resonate because the audience does not know what they're talking about.

Four Stories to Tell

Let's look at four different stories that you can tell. Every story should have a beginning, a middle and an end. It is usually a story about how somebody who had a problem, overcame it and there was an outcome.

The four main stories that you can use are:

1. The listener's story
2. A story about yourself with which people can identify with
3. A story about someone else which people can identify with
4. A shocking story

Let's look at these now.

1. Listeners Story

In this example, we are telling people their story. You can incorporate this when you are speaking to people by describing what they are experiencing at this moment or in the past or as part of their journey. This is powerful because when somebody accepts one suggestion that you give them, then they are more likely to accept the next one. The brain likes to verify everything that you're saying and after a while, stops critically evaluating and accepts more of what you're saying. It's the same for the "yes set". Let's look at an example. Suppose that you were talking about a new product or service and you are presenting it to a group of people.

You could use phrases such as:

> *"Many of you may be wondering about what we're going to be covering today. And you may have been at talks before where there have been big promises made. You may have been at presentations, talks or meetings where there were hundreds of slides, many of which were confusing and written in size 6 font".*

Many people will have experienced this before. The last comment about size 6 font will usually generate a laugh as well.

When you are speaking to people, try to think about what they would have experienced before and use the story to build up a rapport with them.

2 A Story about Yourself

The second type of story is where you relate a story about yourself. The secret when doing this is to make the story about yourself but something with which the other person or an audience can identify. You will see a lot of marketers do this and they will tell their story, which is a story that the audience can identify with and may have experienced.

3. Someone Else's Story

The third story is the "my friend John technique". This is very effective in the world of persuasion and influence. "When we tell a story about someone else", people will automatically put themselves in the role of the person that you are describing. This is a way of communicating to people and getting them to do something without actually telling them.

Let's suppose that the person you're talking to does not have any house insurance. If you were to tell them, they should have house insurance, they may resist. People resist what they are told and they accept what they conclude. If we know they don't have any house insurance, we can use a story. With the story, we described what has happened to somebody else and the consequences of not renewing their house insurance. This is a subtle but powerful way to get people to do what you want, particularly if you can engage the senses and the emotional part of the brain. We are not telling the person what to do but allowing them to conclude it themself.

4. Shock Story

If you know that an objection may come up to something that you are talking about and you want to overcome this, you can use a story to do so. Sometimes people need a shock to get them thinking. I'm going to share with you a story that I heard years ago, which was very effective. The point here is not to judge whether this is in the best taste, but to show the power of stories.

The story concerns a financial adviser who used a shock tactic to sell life assurance. With accidental death, no one thinks it will happen to them. The financial advisor, when discussing life assurance, would say to a couple:

"We've just received some tragic news that John, your husband, has been killed in a road accident."

The financial adviser would look at the wife and ask: "What are you going to do about the children?" The husband would interject.

"We could always ask your sister and see if she would look after them."

The financial advisor would then turn to him and say:

"I'm sorry we can't hear you, you're no longer with us."

Sometimes a shock tactic is needed to change perspective.

Real or Borrowed Stories

Use actual stories and not made up ones. It is useful to record useful stories and have a repository or swipe file for use whenever needed.

Going Sailing

Another useful way to communicate your message is to use similes and metaphors. Metaphors compare something to something else to aid understanding.

Let's just suppose that we were selling investment products and we said to somebody a particular investment is low volatile investment. Now, what does that mean? It's very difficult to construct a picture of that and remember we think in pictures. We could do this a different way and say:

"This investment strategy is a low volatile investment strategy."

We then use a rhetorical question as we covered earlier and ask what is a low volatile investment strategy. We may say:

"You may be wondering what a low volatile investment strategy is."

We can then use a metaphor (using something to illustrate something else):

Imagine (this triggers imagination) that we were going to go out sailing on the sea. Some of us prefer to know that the sea is going to be calm and predictable as we are not looking for any surprises or thrills.

However, other people want to go out in the rough seas with the enormous waves where they will get the unpredictability, thrills and excitement and take the risk that goes with it.

Our investment strategy it's more like sailing in a calm sea. You won't get nasty surprises. The investment ride is smoother and more predictable, making for a more comfortable investment journey.

This would work much better than explaining that an investment has a volatility of two versus another investment that has a volatility of eight.

Telling a Bad Story

While telling a good story is very effective, telling a bad one can have the opposite effect. It is the message in the story that is important, not the details. Let's give an example:

"Last Wednesday when I was travelling to Edinburgh or was it Tuesday, no it can't have been Tuesday because on Tuesday I had to go to the doctors and then I had the electrician coming round to fix the socket, no it was definitely Wednesday."

By now people will think, will you just get to the point! Remember to keep your stories relevant, engage the senses and embed the message that you want within them and get to the point!

CHAPTER 24

Conclusion

The degree to which you can communicate well and speak to people will affect your success in your business, personal and intimate relationships. No one is born an excellent communicator. This has to be learned and many of the "natural communicators" that you may have witnessed have had hours of practise refining their skills.

The brain is constantly changing and adapting. We learned how people are wired, how they think, and how they react. We have focussed on how to talk to people in any situation using proven principles and how to take advantage of hard wired biases within us all. We have explored the importance of state control using "R+", how to use the heart with the heart trigger, the power of words, building rapport and how to structure a conversation with anyone, anytime and in any situation. We learned how to use questions to gain power in any situation and how to create authority. We finished with different types of stories and how to convey a message within a story. If you follow the material in this book, you have all the tools to become a masterful communicator. Break it down into small chunks and practise. Master a skill and then move on. Don't confine this book to gathering dust, but come back to it frequently and notice the impact that it has on your life. The rest is up to you. You can do it and I look forward to your success!

Get Your Complimentary

BONUS Rapid Learning Accelerator Audio
&
BONUS Chapter "Seating for Power & Influence"

https://www.talktoanybodybook.com

Thank you for reading this book.

It would be enormously helpful if you would be kind enough to leave a review because it helps authors.

Many thanks, I appreciate it.

Coaching, Training & Speaking Enquiries

www.power2mind.com

Please see the next page for other books by the author

Other Books by the Author

References

Backster, C., 2003. *Primary perception*. Anza: White rose millennium Press.

", R. (1976). *The structure of magic*. Palo Alto, CA: Science and Behavior Books.

Bandler, R., Grinder, J., & Andreas, S. (1990). *Frogs into princes: Neuro Linguistic Programming*. London: Eden Grove.

Bandler, R., Grinder, J., & Andreas, S. (1994). *Reframing: neuro-linguistic programming and the transformation of meaning*. Moab Utah: Real People Press.

Bandler, R., Grinder, J., & DeLozier, J. (1996). *Patterns of the hypnotic techniques of Milton H. Erickson, M.D.* Scotts Valley, CA: Grinder & Associates.

Bandler, R. (2008). *Richard Bandlers guide to trance-formation*. Deerfield Beach, FL: Health Communications, Inc.

Birdwhistell, R. L. (1971). *Kinesics and context: Essays on body-motion communication*. London.

Bolstad, R. (2011). *Resolve: a new model of therapy*. Carmarthen, Wales: Crown House Pub.

Borthwick, D., 2020. Inside the Mind of Sales. Derek Borthwick.Amazon

Borthwick, D., 2021. How to Read Any Body. Derek Borthwick.Amazon

Brown, D. (2007). *Tricks of the mind*. London: Channel 4 Books.

Bruce Lipton https://www.brucelipton.com/category/topics/new-biology

Childre, D. L., Atkinson, M., McCraty, R., & Tomasino, D. (2001). *Science of the heart: exploring the role of the heart*. Boulder Creek, CA: HeartMath Research Center, Institute of HearMath.

Cialdini, R. B. (2007). *Influence: the psychology of persuasion: Robert B. Cialdini*. New York: Collins.

Cialdini, R. B. (2018). *Pre-suasion: a revolutionary way to influence and persuade*. New York: Simon & Schuster Paperbacks.

Clark, B. C., Mahato, N. K., Nakazawa, M., Law, T. D., & Thomas, J. S. (2014). The power of the mind: the cortex as a critical determinant of muscle strength/weakness. *Journal of Neurophysiology, 112*(12), 3219–3226. doi: 10.1152/jn.00386.2014

Clark, L. V. (1960). Effect of Mental Practice on the Development of a Certain Motor Skill. *Research Quarterly. American Association for Health, Physical Education and Recreation, 31*(4), 560–569. doi: 10.1080/10671188.1960.10613109

Covey, S. R. (2016). *The 7 habits of highly effective people*. San Francisco, CA: FranklinCovey Co.

Cuddy, A. J. C., Schultz, S. J., & Fosse, N. E. (2018). P-Curving a More Comprehensive Body of Research on Postural Feedback Reveals Clear Evidential Value for Power-Posing Effects: Reply to Simmons and Simonsohn (2017). *Psychological Science, 29*(4), 656–666. doi: 10.1177/0956797617746749

Dantalion, J. (2008). *Mind Control Language Patterns*. Lieu de publication inconnu: Mind Control Publishing.

Dawson, R. (2014, October 14). The Secrets of Power Negotiating. Retrieved from https://www.audible.com/pd/The-Secrets-of-Power-Negotiating-Audiobook/B00NMQVS9G

Eagleman, D. (2012). *Incognito*. Rearsby: Clipper Large Print.

Eagleman, D., n.d. *Livewired*.

Elman, D. (1970). *Hypnotherapy*. Glendale, CA: Westwood Pub. Co.

Emoto, M., 2005. *The true power of water*. Hillsboro, Ore.: Beyond Words Pub.

Estabrooks, G. H. (1968). *Hypnotism*. New York: Dutton.

Grinder, J., & Bandler, R. (1985). *Trance-formations: neuro-linguistic programming and the structure of hypnosis*. Moab: Real People Press.

Hall, E. (2018). *Strongman: my story*. London: Virgin Books.

Heller, S., & Steele, T. L. (2009). *Monsters & magical sticks: there's no such thing as hypnosis?* Tempe, AZ: Original Falcon Press.

Cedar Books. (1988). *How to win friends and influence people*. London.

Hull, C. L. (1968). *Hypnosis and suggestibility An experimental approach*. New York: Appleton-Century-Crofts.

Jung, C. (2016). Psychological Types. doi: 10.4324/9781315512334

Kimbro, D. P., Hill, N., & Hill, N. (1997). *Think and grow rich: a Black choice*. New York: Fawcett Columbine.

Klaff, O. (2011). *Pitch anything: an innovative method for presenting, persuading and winning the deal*. New York, NY: McGraw-Hill.

Klopfer, B. (1957). Psychological Variables In Human Cancer. *Journal of Projective Techniques, 21*(4), 331–340. doi: 10.1080/08853126.1957.10380794

Knox, R. (2014, January 10). Half Of A Drug's Power Comes From Thinking It Will Work. Retrieved June 16, 2020, from https://www.npr.org/sections/health-shots/2014/01/10/261406721/half-a-drugs-power-comes-from-thinking-it-will-work

Koch, R. (1998). *80/20 Principle: the secret of achieving more with less. (Alternate title: Eighty-twenty principle)*. New York: Currency.

Kolenda, N. (2013). *Methods of persuasion: how to use psychology to influence human behavior*. Place of publication not identified: publisher not identified.

Ledochowski, I. (2003). *The deep trance training manual*. Carmarthen, Wales: Crown House Pub.

Lorayne, H. (1979). *How to develop a super-power memory*. Wellingborough: A. Thomas.

Macknik, S. L., Martinez-Conde, S., & Blakeslee, S. (2012). *Sleights of mind: what the neuroscience of magic reveals about our brains*. London: Profile.

Maclean, P. D. (1988). Triune Brain. *Comparative Neuroscience and Neurobiology*, 126–128. doi: 10.1007/978-1-4899-6776-3_51

McGill, O. (1947). *The encyclopedia of genuine stage hypnotism*. Colon, MI: Abbotts Magic Novelty Co.

Michael H., M. I., C., G., & Volker. (2014, September 29). Neurobiological foundations of neurologic music therapy: rhythmic entrainment and the motor system.

Milgram, S. (1963). Behavioral study of obedience. *Journal of Abnormal and Social Psychology*, 67, 371-378.

Miller, G. A. (1956). The magical number seven, plus or minus two: some limits on our capacity for processing information. *Psychological Review*, *63*(2), 81–97. doi: 10.1037/h0043158

Murphy, J. (2013). *The power of your subconscious mind, Dr. Joseph Murphy*. Place of publication not identified: Wildside Press.

Myrvold, Wayne, Marco Genovese, and Abner Shimony, "Bell's Theorem", *The Stanford Encyclopedia of Philosophy* (Fall 2021 Edition), Edward N. Zalta (ed.)
Navarro, J., & Karlins, M. (2015). *What every Body is saying: an ex-Fbi agents guide to speed-reading people*. New York, NY: Harper Collins.

OBrien, D. (1994). *How to develop a perfect memory*. London: Headline.

Pascual-Leone, A., Nguyet, D., Cohen, L. G., Brasil-Neto, J. P., Cammarota, A., & Hallett, M. (1995). Modulation of muscle responses evoked by transcranial magnetic stimulation during the acquisition of new fine motor skills. *Journal of Neurophysiology*, *74*(3), 1037–1045. doi: 10.1152/jn.1995.74.3.1037

Pease, A. (1997). *How to read others thoughts by their gestures*. London: Sheldon.

Pulos, L. (2014, October 14). The Biology of Empowerment. Retrieved from https://www.audible.com/pd/The-Biology-of-Empowerment-Audiobook/B0OO3I9V8M

Rossi, E. L. (1993). *The psychobiology of mind-body healing: new concepts of therapeutic hypnosis*. New York: Norton.

NLP power Dr. David Snyder. Retrieved from https://www.youtube.com/user/SanDiegoKarate

NLP power https://www.nlppower.com/product/killer-influence/

Schmidt, H. (1970). A quantum mechanical random number generator for psi tests. *Journal of Parapsychology*, *34*, 219-224.

Schmidt, H. (1970). Mental influence on random events. *New Scientist & Science Journal, 50*, 757-758.

Syed, M. (2010). *How champions are made*. London: Fourth Estate.

Talbot, M. (1991). *The holographic universe*. London: Grafton Books.
Endel Tulving. Elements of Episodic Memory. Oxford, Clarendon [U.A, 2007.
Tversky, A., & Kahneman, D. (1974). Judgment under Uncertainty: Heuristics and Biases. *Science, 185*(4157), 1124–1131. doi: 10.1126/science.185.4157.1124

Watson, J. B. (1913). Psychology as the behaviorist views it. *Psychological Review, 20*(2), 158–177. doi: 10.1037/h0074428

Welch, C. (2015). *How the art of medicine makes the science more effective: becoming the medicine we practice*. London: Singing Dragon.

Wendy A. Suzuki, Mónica I. Feliú-Mójer, Uri Hasson, Rachel Yehuda and Jean Mary Zarate Journal of Neuroscience 31 October 2018, JNEUROSCI.1942-18.2018

9 781838 33